Data for Journalists

This straightforward and effective how-to guide provides the basics for any reporter or journalism student beginning to use data for news stories. It has step-by-step instructions on how to do basic data analysis in journalism while addressing why these digital tools should be an integral part of reporting in the 21st century. In an ideal core text for courses on data-driven journalism or computer-assisted reporting, Houston emphasizes that journalists are accountable for the accuracy and relevance of the data they acquire and share.

With a refreshed design, this updated new edition includes expanded coverage on social media, scraping data from the web, and text-mining, and provides journalists with the tips and tools they need for working with data.

Brant Houston is a Professor and the Knight Chair in Investigative Reporting at the University of Illinois, where he teaches journalism and oversees an online newsroom. An award-winning journalist, he was an investigative reporter at U.S. newspapers for 17 years. For more than a decade, he served as executive director of Investigative Reporters and Editors, a now 6,000-member association headquartered at the University of Missouri School of Journalism, where he also taught investigative and data reporting. Houston has conducted more than 400 seminars for professional journalists and students in 30 countries, and he is a co-founder of networks of nonprofit newsrooms and educators throughout the world.

D1600025

Data for Journalists

A Practical Guide
for Computer-Assisted
Reporting

Fifth Edition

Brant Houston

Routledge
Taylor & Francis Group

NEW YORK AND LONDON

Fifth edition published 2019
by Routledge
711 Third Avenue, New York, NY 10017

and by Routledge
2 Park Square, Milton Park, Abingdon, Oxon, OX14 4RN

Routledge is an imprint of the Taylor & Francis Group, an informa business

First edition published by St Martin's Press 1996
Fourth edition published by Routledge 2015

Library of Congress Cataloging-in-Publication Data
Names: Houston, Brant, author. | Houston, Brant. Computer-assisted
reporting.
Title: Data for journalists : a practical guide for computer-assisted
reporting / Brant Houston.
Description: Fifth edition. | London ; New York : Routledge, 2019. |
Previous editions titled: Computer-assisted reporting. |
Includes bibliographical references and index.
Identifiers: LCCN 2018031648 (print) | LCCN 2018040823 (ebook) |
ISBN 9781351249317 (ebook) | ISBN 9780815370345 |
ISBN 9780815370345 (hardback :alk. paper) |
ISBN 9780815370406 (paperback :alk. paper) | ISBN 978135124931 7 (ebk)
Subjects: LCSH: Computer-assisted reporting. | Journalism—Data processing.
Classification: LCC PN4784.E5 (ebook) | LCC PN4784.E5 H68 2019 (print) |
DDC 070.40285—dc23
LC record available at https://lccn.loc.gov/2018031648

ISBN: 978-0-8153-7034-5 (hbk)
ISBN: 978-0-8153-7040-6 (pbk)
ISBN: 978-1-351-24931-7 (ebk)

Typeset in Palatino and New York
by Florence Production Ltd, Stoodleigh, Devon, UK

Contents

List of Boxes   xi
Preface   xiii
Features   xv
New to This Edition   xvii
Acknowledgments   xix

1. **What Data Journalism and Computer-Assisted
   Reporting Is and Why Journalists Use It**   1
   The Fundamentals Remain   2
   How to Learn: Trial and Error—and Repetition   11
   Where You Are Going   11
   A Final Thought   14
   Chapter Summary   15
   Applying CAR   15
   Suggested Exercises   16

Part I: Learning Computer-Assisted Reporting Skills

2. **Online Resources: Researching and Finding Data
   on the Internet**   19
   Finding Data   21
   Digital Information and Data on the Internet   23
   Using Online Resources   23
   What Online Resources to Use   24
   Digital Library Researchers and Journalists   25
   Newsroom Databases   25
   Discussion Groups and Social Media   25

Using Boolean Logic to Search the Internet 26
Downloading Databases 27
Downloading Different Files 29
Web Scraping 37
Chapter Summary 39
Applying CAR 40
Suggested Exercises 41

3. **Gathering and Analyzing Text and Social Media** **43**
Social Media for News Gathering and Analysis 50
Crowd-Sourcing 56
Authenticity and Accuracy 57
Chapter Summary 57
Applying CAR 57
Suggested Exercises 58

4. **Spreadsheets, Part 1: Basic Math for Journalists** **59**
Becoming Friendly with Numbers 60
Learning Addresses 62
Calculating Percentages 64
Going from Horizontal to Vertical 67
Comparing Parts to the Sum 69
Sorting the Results 71
Using Average and Median for Better Accuracy 74
Interpreting Outliers 76
Chapter Summary 77
Applying CAR 77
Suggested Exercises 78

5. **Spreadsheets, Part 2: More Math that Matters** **79**
Rates 80
Ranking 84
Filtering 86
Ratios 89
Pivot Tables 90
Graphs and Charts 97
Chapter Summary 100
Applying CAR 100
Suggested Exercises 101

6. **Database Managers, Part 1: Searching and Summarizing**   **103**
The Query   109
Selecting and Searching   112
Criteria and Filtering   113
Sorting   114
Criteria and Wildcards   114
Boolean Logic: And, Or, Not   116
Grouping   118
Chapter Summary   121
Applying CAR   121
Suggested Exercises   122

7. **Database Managers, Part 2: Matchmaking**   **123**
Relational Databases Are Everywhere   124
Joining Tables   125
Enterprise Matchmaking   127
Chapter Summary   131
Applying CAR   132
Suggested Exercises   132

Part II: Using Computer-Assisted Reporting in News Stories

8. **Getting Data Not on the Web: How to Find and Negotiate for Data**   **135**
Finding Data   136
Obtaining a Database   139
The Record Layout   140
Privacy and Security Issues   142
High Costs   143
Importing   144
Chapter Summary   146
Applying CAR   146
Suggested Exercises   147

9. **Building Your Own Database: How to Develop Exclusive Sources**   **149**
When to Build   152
Spreadsheet or Database Manager   153

Using the Database Manager 154
Creating a Relational Database 156
Chapter Summary 158
Applying CAR 158
Suggested Exercises 159

10. Dirty Data: How to Fact Check Your Data and Clean It 161
Never Trust the Data 163
Two Rules 165
Record Layout 166
Record Layout Miscues 166
Cryptic Codes 168
Sorry, Wrong Number 170
Where Is the Standard? 171
Header-Aches 173
Numbers Versus Text 175
Offensive Characters 175
Chapter Summary 176
Applying CAR 177
Suggested Exercises 177

11. Doing the Data Journalism and Computer-Assisted Reporting Story: How to Report and Write with Data 179
Pick a Story You Know Can Be Done 180
Pick a Database You Can Get 181
Some First-Time Examples 181
Start Small 182
Building Your Own 183
Match the Database to Your Knowledge 183
The Minimum Story 184
Keep Up with Other Reporters' Work 185
Integrate Databases into Your Daily Work 185
Find a Partner 186
Become Familiar with the Field of Data Programming 186
Look for Tips 186
Writing the Story 187
Good Reporting and Ethics 188
Stay Curious, Get Excited 188

Chapter Summary   190
Applying CAR   190
Suggested Exercises   191

Appendix A: A Short Introduction to Mapping Data   193
Appendix B: A Short Introduction to Social Network
                    Analysis   205
Selected Bibliography   215
Websites   217
Sources for Key Examples   219
Glossary   221
Index   225

Boxes

Chapter 1
Box 1.1: History of Computer-Assisted Reporting   7
Box 1.2: The Basic Tools and the Advanced Tools   9

Chapter 2
Box 2.1: Purposes of Online Resources   21
Box 2.2: Different File Types   28

Chapter 3
Box 3.1: Open Calais   47
Box 3.2: Kinds of Social Media   50
Box 3.3: Useful Tools for Searching Social Media   52

Chapter 6
Box 6.1: Purposes of a Database Manager   104
Box 6.2: The Six Commands   110

Chapter 8
Box 8.1: Steps for Finding Data   136
Box 8.2: Three Levels of Sources   138
Box 8.3: Parts of the Record Layout   140
Box 8.4: Fair Price   143

Chapter 9
Box 9.1: The Checklist for Building a Database   153

Chapter 10
Box 10.1: Lessons Learned   164
Box 10.2: Kinds of Pitfalls   165

Chapter 11
Box 11.1: Building Your Own Database over Time   180
Box 11.2: Reporting With CAR   189

Preface

It has been more than three decades since I began using databases in my reporting and two decades since I began writing the first edition of this book.

During those 32 years, software and hardware have constantly changed and evolved and, over time, have become much simpler to use. Heavy data analysis can be done on a laptop or desktop, online, or in the Cloud. Results can be rapidly visualized and shared across the internet and the public can contribute to the creation of a database.

Meanwhile, the number of journalists using digital techniques and data has risen dramatically. A new generation of programmers and coders has joined newsrooms and journalists in analyzing data, bringing with them a fresh viewpoint and the skills to better visualize data and make it interactive.

Yet the need for a guide to help those just beginning to use databases for reporting purposes has not lessened. If anything, the demand has increased, as working journalists and journalism students realize the importance of obtaining the basic skills and the knowledge to use databases to create meaningful news stories through accurate analysis.

In journalism, finding interesting data, visualizing it, and presenting it in a pleasing format is not enough. Today's news audience wants to know what the databases reveal and mean and what analysis of the data says about whether systems and policies are working, and society is being served. Many readers, viewers, and listeners seldom have the time to do their own data analysis or to follow through with the interviews and street work that must go along with such analysis.

Thus, the purpose of this textbook remains the same as when I first wrote it: to provide a practical guide that is based not on a fascination with data or programming but instead focuses on coupling analysis with traditional reporting to produce more in-depth, more profound, and more useful journalism.

This book also is a product of my teaching the basics of computer-assisted reporting (CAR) in hundreds of seminars and conferences around the world. The evolution of this text also continues to benefit from listening to suggestions from students, teachers, journalists, and other readers. The result is a blending of a step-by-step approach to using software—an approach that never forgets that data, software, and analysis are all being implemented for better journalism.

The fifth edition of *Computer-Assisted Reporting* still provides students with advice on the data collection and analysis skills they need for news stories. The basics of CAR—finding and using data on the internet, employing spreadsheets and/or database managers to analyze data, building your own databases, cleaning dirty data, and visualizing the data—can help any journalist or student working with data achieve greater speed and insight. The basics can also help journalists and students discover, substantiate, and write successful stories on subjects they had not imagined before.

This guide also addresses and stresses the need for accuracy in data analysis. While crowd-sourcing during reporting or after publication has proven extremely helpful, publishing an authoritative story first online with significant errors and then correcting through crowdsourcing does not really work. From the start, a journalist needs to be credible and keep errors to a minimum. Otherwise, journalism becomes just another voice of unverified information or "fake news" that lacks credibility or authority—and makes a journalist vulnerable to a lawsuit.

For the classroom or seminar, *Computer-Assisted Reporting* can be used as a core text or a supplement to any introductory or intermediate journalism textbook. Enhancing this edition also is valuable supplementary material on the web.

Features

Because CAR is only as good as the stories it produces, the fifth edition includes reporting and writing advice for using CAR skills in daily and beat reporting. Other key features of *Computer-Assisted Reporting* have been retained and updated as needed. They include:

- A practical approach that helps students master the basics, teaching them essential skills they need in concise, accessible language.
- Screenshots from software commonly used in journalism, such as Microsoft Excel and Access, DB Browser for SQLite, and Google tools, which let students match what they see in the book to what they see on their screens and confirm their results.
- Real-life examples of news stories using CAR techniques, including both classics and new hits.
- "Your Turn to Practice" exercises that provide realistic and engaging assignments that give students the chance to practice the skills they have learned.

New to This Edition

To keep pace with the changing journalistic practices and help students clearly see how to apply CAR skills, material in this fifth edition will be linked with online resources at Investigative Reporters and Editors (IRE), the National Institute of Computer-Assisted Reporting (NICAR), and the Global Investigative Journalism Network to provide more exercises and tutorials online.

Other changes include:

- Exercises in spreadsheets and database managers that use more recent versions of Microsoft and free products.
- An updated chapter on researching, using, and downloading data found online.
- A new chapter on using unstructured data and social media, as well as the basics of web scraping.
- Special online exercises and data relevant to international journalists.

Acknowledgments

I thank IRE, NICAR, and the Global Investigative Journalism Network for their continued support for CAR and for conferences held over the years that keep professionals, professors, and students up to date with ever-changing technology and techniques. In particular, my thanks go out to long-time colleague in CAR, Nils Mulvad; and former and current NICAR trainers Sarah Cohen, David Donald, Jaimi Dowdell, David Herzog, Jennifer LaFleur, Denise Malan, Jo Craven McGinty, Tom McGinty, Richard Mullins, Ron Nixon, Aron Pilhofer, Jeff Porter, and Neil Reisner.

I also appreciate the help provided by my former students over the years—now accomplished journalists—in the development of previous editions. Those students include Jack Dolan, Justin Mayo, John Sullivan and MaryJo Webster. Foremost, I acknowledge the guidance and work of my mentors and pioneers in using data for journalism—Steve Doig, Elliot Jaspin, Philip Meyer, and Dwight Morris.

My thanks also goes to my current editor Erica Wetter, who encouraged me to do this fifth edition and has patiently supported its development and publication.

And, again my deepest thanks to my wife, Rhonda, and to my parents. They have always given their full support for my work in journalism and that support has made all the difference.

One final word. Despite the expanding power and breadth of CAR, it remains only a tool for journalists. It aids, but does not replace, the imagination, experience, interviewing skills, intuition, skepticism, fieldwork, and passion of the dedicated journalist, who I acknowledge last but not least.

What Data Journalism and Computer-Assisted Reporting Is and Why Journalists Use It

Journalists need to be data-savvy. It used to be that you would get stories by chatting to people in bars, and it still might be that you'll do it that way some times. But now it's also going to be about poring over data and equipping yourself with the tools to analyze it and picking out what's interesting. And keeping it in perspective, helping people out by really seeing where it all fits together, and what's going on in the country.

—Tim Berners-Lee, creator of the
World Wide Web (2010)

The open question in 2014 is not whether data, computers, and algorithms can be used by journalists in the public interest, but rather how, when, where, why, and by whom. Today, journalists can treat all of that data as a source, interrogating it for answers as they would a human.

—Alexander Benjamin Howard, *The Art and
Science of Data-Driven Journalism* (2014)

While **computer-assisted reporting** (CAR) has been much more widely practiced since the 1980s, it is since the beginning of the 21st century that the critical importance of journalists having the ability to analyze and visualize data has been globally recognized.

Fortunately, during the same time, it has become much easier to do. Many software tools have become simpler to use. A rich variety of data is now online and often very simple to **download**.

Storage space is immense on hard drives, flash drives, and in the cloud. The computing power on a laptop, tablet, or mobile phone dwarfs the power available only a few years ago.

The ways to visualize data for better understanding and analysis are numerous and increasing. Furthermore, a wave of computer programmers/coders has joined with journalists to tackle the problems of capturing data from the web, cleaning and organizing it, and creating fascinating interactive presentations to be shared with the public and that encourage citizen participation and analysis.

However, many fundamental truths remain. **Databases** are created by people—or by programs created by people. Thus, databases have errors and omissions that people have made and those flaws must be noted and corrected. Every database also is a slice in time and thus, potentially outdated the moment it is acquired and used.

Also remember that a database alone is not journalism. It is a field of information that needs to be harvested carefully with insight and caution. It needs to be compared and augmented with **observation** and interviews.

It is still important to determine the accuracy of a database before using it. Equally important is the careful analysis of a database since one small error can result in monstrously wrong conclusions. The idea of uploading data on the web and hoping the public or volunteers will consistently make sense of it with reliable analysis has proven unreliable. In fact, journalists—not advocates—are needed more than ever to deliver a well-researched understanding of information and data, and to write and visualize a compelling story.

The Fundamentals Remain

Despite changes in technology and the availability of mega-data, some scenarios have not changed.

For example, as a local reporter in the United States, you may want to look into how many inmates are in jails because they do not have the money for bail, which means they are in jail until trial. You see that a recent audit of jails points out that many persons are in jail not because they have been convicted, but because they simply do not have the finances to pay the bail set for them. Furthermore, it appears anecdotally that judges are setting higher bails for black and Hispanic males than white males.

With a little research, you find that the county jails keep records on inmates that include the amount of bail in each case, the charges against the inmate, and each inmate's race and gender. After a series of meetings, the officials will agree to give you the database with the information you need. Irritatingly, they do not want to put it online for you to retrieve, but they will give you a DVD containing the database.

By the next day, you do your first analysis of the data and see that the bail for black and Hispanics males is often double that for white males, even when they are charged with the same crime and have the same criminal and personal background. Over the next few weeks, you check through the records and gather more details. You recheck your information, look at other documents, conduct interviews, and write the story. The work culminates in a significant article that presents a systematic look at justice gone wrong. The best weak answer the officials have is the system discriminates against the poor, not just blacks and Hispanics.

Or consider another scenario: you want to know how weak security is at your nearby metropolitan airport. So you get local police reports or download recent information from the Transportation Security Administration about dangerous materials seized as passengers go through security. You begin analyzing the database, which consists of counting the number of violations at local airports in recent years and then examining closely the details of those violations.

You quickly find serious and surprising violations in which guns, knives, and other weapons are seized. You follow up with research on the web and interviews with airport officials, law enforcement, and airline companies. You review reports by government investigators posted on the web. Within days, you have an important story that the public needs to know.

In fact, more than 100 news organizations used local police databases while doing airport security stories in the weeks, months, and years following the terrorists' attacks in the United States on September 11, 2001. More recently, journalism students at Medill wrote this very story and created an online database to go with it.

On a more immense and global scale, consider this example:

> A newsroom receives a leak of a millions of documents revealing the use of offshore bank accounts by the wealthy or international criminals.
>
> Rather than simply post the documents to an online site, the newsroom carefully reviews the authenticity of the data, converts it from unstructured data (text) to structured data that can be analyzed and visualized, and then shares it with hundreds of journalists across the world to report and verify on the data before publishing a word.

This has actually happened several times in the past decade at the International Consortium of Investigative Journalists, a non-profit newsroom in Washington D.C.

At the base of these techniques is a practice known as CAR—also called **data journalism**—which is often the place to begin if you are a journalist without computer science background. As you will learn in this book, CAR has become a part of everyday journalism. Journalists use these and other techniques for daily reporting, beat reporting, and for the large projects that win national and international awards. In the last two decades, journalism awards have gone to the International Consortium for Investigative Journalism for its investigations using big data leaks; *The Washington Post* for stories on police shootings and child abuse; and to the small newspaper, the *Bristol* (Virginia) *Herald Courier*, for the work of reporter Daniel Gilbert who built and used a database as part of his investigation into natural-gas royalties owed to thousands of landowners in southwest Virginia.

CAR does not refer to journalists sitting at a keyboard writing stories or surfing the web and social media. It refers to downloading or building databases and doing data analysis that can provide context and depth to daily stories. It refers to techniques of producing tips that launch more complex stories from a broader perspective and with a better understanding of the issues. A journalist beginning a story with the knowledge of the patterns gleaned from 150,000 court records is way ahead of a reporter who sees only a handful of court cases each week.

The techniques of CAR do not replace proven journalistic practices. It has become a part of them. It also requires greater responsibility and vigilance. The old standard—"verify, verify, verify"—that one learns in basic reporting classes becomes more critical. "Healthy skepticism" becomes ever more important. The idea of interviewing multiple sources and cross-referencing them becomes ever more crucial.

"Computers don't make a bad reporter into a good reporter. What they do is make a good reporter better," Elliot Jaspin, one of the pioneers in CAR, said three decades ago.

Many practicing journalists have sought training in the past three decades and become proficient in the basic skills of CAR. They have overcome computer and math phobia, and they now put these skills to use on a daily basis, leading to more precision and sophistication in their reporting.

To quote Philip Meyer, another pioneer in database analysis for news stories, "They are raising the ante on what it takes to be journalist."

Aiding in the progress and acceptance of these skills has been the proliferation of the web and social media, the development of inexpensive and easy-to-use computers and software, the increased attention to the value of data and techniques of data and visual analysis in newsrooms, and the use of **algorithms** in finding patterns and creating content.

CAR and the other approaches to data—such as precision journalism or **computational journalism**—are no longer a sidebar to mainstream journalism. They are essential to surviving as a journalist in the 21st century. The digital tools won't replace a good journalist's imagination, the ability to conduct revealing interviews, or the talent to develop human sources. But a journalist who knows how to use analytical and visual software in day-to-day and long-term work will gather and analyze information more quickly, and develop and deliver a deeper understanding. The journalist will be better prepared for interviews and be able to write with more authority. That journalist also will see potential stories that would have never occurred to him or her.

That journalist also achieves parity with politicians, bureaucrats, advocates, and business people who have enjoyed many advantages over the journalists simply because they had the money and knowledge to utilize databases and digital information before journalists did. Government officials and workers have long been comfortable entering information into computers and then retrieving and analyzing it. Businesses, small and large, routinely use spreadsheet and database software. Advocacy groups frequently employ databases to push their agendas.

Without a rudimentary knowledge of the advantages and disadvantages of data analysis, it is difficult for the contemporary journalist to fully understand and report on how the world now works. And it is far more difficult for a journalist to do meaningful public service journalism or to perform the necessary watchdog role.

As long ago as 1990, Frank Daniels III, former executive editor of *The Raleigh News & Observer*, recognized the challenge. He began his newspaper's early and oft-lauded push into CAR because the 1990 campaign of then Senator Jesse Helms was profoundly more computer-sophisticated than Daniels's own newspaper. "It made me realize how stupid we were, and I don't like feeling stupid," Daniels recalled.

Daniels was right about the bad position in which journalists had put themselves. For years, journalists were like animals in a zoo, waiting to be fed pellets of information by the keepers who are happy for journalists to stay in their Luddite cages. But a good journalist always wants to see original information because every time someone else selects or sorts that information, they can add spin or bias, which sometimes can't be detected. CAR can help prevent that from happening.

Many journalists and journalism students now learn the basic tools of CAR because they realize that it is the best way to get to the information because most governmental and commercial records are now stored electronically. Despite security concerns and efforts to keep information secret, there still are a mind-boggling and growing number of databases on U.S. and international websites. So without the ability to deal with electronic data, a journalist is cut off from some of the best, untainted information. The old-fashioned journalist will never get to the information on time—or worse, will be brutally trampled by the competing data savvy media.

For a journalist or journalism student, this knowledge also is crucial in the competition to getting a good job. At many news organizations, an applicant that has these skills—which are far more than the ability to search the web or use social media—gets his or her resume moved to the top of the list.

A journalist does not have to be a programmer or someone who knows software code, although that also can make a huge difference. But a journalist who can use a **spreadsheet** or **database manager** is free to thoroughly explore information, reexamine it, and reconsider what it means in relation to interviews and observations in the field. The journalist can take the "spin" off the information and get closer to the truth. A journalist may not be a statistician, but a good journalist knows enough about statistics to know how easy it is to manipulate them or lie with them. In the same way, if a journalist understands how data can be manipulated, he or she can better judge a bureaucrat's spin on the facts or a government's misuse of a database.

Journalists have found, too, that if they let a government employee whose job is only to process data and do basic analysis, the results may be incomplete, or hide the nuances or potential pitfalls of the data. The conscientious journalist also does not want to fall into a cycle of asking for a report in some static digital format, studying the report, coming up with more questions, and then asking for another report. Why get into a lengthy back-and-forth when you can engage in a rapid, multidimensional conversation with the full dataset on your computer screen?

Most important, CAR is at the heart of public service journalism and of vigilant daily community reporting. This is true whether writing about education, business, government, environment issues, or any other topic.

BOX 1.1 **History of Computer-Assisted Reporting**

Some argue that data has always been a part of journalism since there were maps or tables of statistics in newspapers in the 18th or 19th century. But many practitioners and scholars date the beginning of CAR to 1952, when CBS used experts with a mainframe computer to predict the outcome of the presidential election. That's a bit of a stretch, or perhaps it was a false beginning because it wasn't until 1967 that data analysis started to catch on.

continued

In that year, Philip Meyer at *The Detroit Free Press* used a mainframe to analyze a survey of Detroit residents for the purpose of understanding and explaining the serious riots that erupted in the city that summer. Meyer went on to work in the 1970s with *The Philadelphia Inquirer* reporters Donald Barlett and James Steele to analyze the sentencing patterns in the local court system and with Rich Morin at the *Miami Herald* to analyze property assessment records. Meyer also wrote a book called *Precision Journalism* that explained and advocated using database analysis and social research methods in reporting. (Several revisions of the book have been published since then.)

Still, only a few journalists used these techniques until the mid-1980s when Elliot Jaspin received recognition while at *The Providence Journal-Bulletin* for analyzing databases for stories, including those on dangerous school bus drivers and on a political scandal involving home loans. Jaspin had learned his skills at Columbia University where professor Steve Ross had begun teaching the use of computers under the term of "analytic journalism."

During the 1980s other journalists across the country, often consulting with Meyer or Jaspin, also began doing data analysis for their stories. Aiding their efforts were improved personal computers and a program—Nine Track Express—that Jaspin and journalist-programmer Daniel Woods wrote to make it easier to transfer computer tapes (that contain nine "tracks" of information) to personal computers using a portable tape drive. This allowed journalists to circumvent the bureaucracies and delays involved in using mainframes.

In 1989, the profession recognized the value of CAR when it gave a Pulitzer Prize to *The Atlanta Journal-Constitution* for its stories on racial disparities in home loan practices. During the same year, Jaspin established the institute at the Missouri School of Journalism now known as the National Institute for CAR (NICAR), and Indiana University professor James Brown established the National Institute for Advanced Reporting and held the first CAR conference in Indianapolis. Since that time use of CAR blossomed, primarily due to the seminars conducted at Missouri and throughout the world by Investigative Reporters and Editors Inc. (IRE) and the NICAR, which is a joint program of IRE and the Missouri School of Journalism. Since 2001, IRE and the Global Investigative Journalism Network, an association of more than 160 nonprofit newsrooms around the world, have greatly expanded the teaching and use of data journalism both online and at its biannual conferences. Among other organizations contributing to the growth of data journalism have been the European conference Data Harvest, Wits University's annual investigative conference in Africa, Google News Labs, and the newspaper, *The Guardian* in the United Kingdom, through its educational services.

In addition, the field of computational journalism, which brings journalists and programmers together, has begun pushing journalists into better understanding algorithms that help with news gathering or to investigate algorithms used by social media companies to segregate people by their interests or backgrounds.

BOX 1.2 **The Basic Tools and the Advanced Tools**

Over time, three basic skills (which are mostly the focus of this book) for CAR have emerged: online resources (primarily finding and downloading databases), spreadsheets, and database managers. As journalists have become more technologically sophisticated, other tools have joined these three, including *statistical software*, geographical information systems (GISs) or *mapping software*, and *social network analysis software.*

Since then, journalists have added such techniques as web **scraping** (automatically downloading individual records from the web and collating them into a database), methods of cleaning and organizing data through programming languages such as Python, and visualizing data in different ways through a program such as Tableau. But in providing training to thousands of journalists since 1989, teachers have often found that the beginning journalist starts most comfortably with the first three tools:

Online resources are available to journalists through a variety of ways. Online resources include (1) email, (2) discussion groups, (3) social media, and (4) active and archived databases, where records are stored. With online resources you can look up court records, retrieve business records or the national census of countries, and find thousands of other databases for nearly every topic, whether local or global. You can also monitor discussion groups, email, and social media for trends and tips.

Spreadsheet software such as Microsoft Excel or Google sheets is good for analyzing numbers. You should think about using a spreadsheet whenever you are looking at salaries, budgets, census data, prices,

continued

or statistical reports. A spreadsheet allows you to quickly filter and sum columns of numbers, compare them, sort them, and put your results into charts. While a spreadsheet can allow you to do much more, these are routine uses for basic CAR.

A *database manager* such as Microsoft Access, DB Brower SQLite, or MySQL is good for searching, summarizing, and joining and relating different files known as **tables**. A database manager can quickly group similar kinds of information and link different files through keywords or identification numbers. It enables you to look up information about a person quickly by name, street address, or phone number. It enables you to look up political contributions to a particular candidate, group those contributions, and total them by number or amount. It enables you to match the names in one file of information, such as death certificates, to names in another file, such as voters. (There's always a potential story when you find dead people voting.)

A database manager also can deftly handle many more records than a spreadsheet, especially when you have several files.

The more advanced tools of CAR are:

Statistical software (the more advanced functions of Excel, SPSS, or SAS are three common tools and R is a popular free open-source software) becomes attractive later when a journalist feels more comfortable with numbers and wants to perform more detailed and robust analysis. Journalists use it for looking at such topics as school testing scores or racial disparities in mortgages or insurance.

GIS or *mapping software* (two of the simpler being Tableau and Google Fusion tables, while the more sophisticated is Arc Online distributed by the company ESRI) illustrates the points made in a story and illuminates disclosures that otherwise would remain unseen. Journalists often use it for election votes, dangerous environmental areas, social media tracking, and many other topics.

A groundbreaking use of mapping software was done by Steve Doig at the *Miami Herald* in the early 1990s, when he exposed shoddy building codes by comparing hurricane wind speeds to building damage. A more recent use was by *The Guardian* newspaper in the United Kingdom, when it mapped the origins of rioters through social media.

Social networking software (ranging from a plug-in to Microsoft Excel called NodeXL, to many free open-source programs such as Gephi) visually draws connections between people and/or organizations. Journalists are beginning to more frequently use this software, and you can see the concepts applied at many newsroom websites. Anthropologists, business consultants, intelligence and police agencies, and health researchers have already used this social network analysis for years to explore relationships.

Natural Language Processing software. (There are many different programs but one common one is Open Calais.) These programs are sophisticated software that help analyze unstructured data (text, photos, and videos) to see patterns, outliers, and categories of information.

Again, this book will concentrate on the basic tools and analysis that can get you going in a classroom or newsroom. This book will strip away the distractions that seem so plentiful when you begin learning how to use software, and it will show you shortcuts to doing effective stories. The book also will put the use of software into the context of journalism and day-to-day reporting.

How to Learn: Trial and Error—and Repetition

The best way to learn CAR is through trial and error. *You have to practice.* You have to make mistakes in asking questions of the information. You need to try different queries in database managers, look at the result, and try again to see if you can better focus your inquiry and the answers to it. You need to be intellectually daring and creative to think of the variables that could affect a conclusion.

The exercises that accompany this book can be found on the web at ijec.org/databook. They will give you plenty of opportunities to try different ways of arranging data and to discover the best way to find valid answers. Moreover, you have to realize that despite all the software advances, computer software still has quirks, multiple icons, and obscure keystrokes. Practice is the way to become more comfortable with the tools.

Where You Are Going

Part 1 of this book, "Learning CAR Skills," concentrates on the basic skills. Part 2, "Using CAR in News Stories," focuses on producing computer-assisted stories and overcoming common newsgathering problems that occur when you use these skills.

The first section concentrates on learning the basic CAR skills for **sorting, filtering,** and summarizing data. These skills include downloading data from websites and importing it into spreadsheets and database managers; using math, charts, and other tools in spreadsheets to analyze data; and using database managers to search, summarize, and compare databases.

In addition, the first section looks at the beginning ways to deal with social media and other unstructured data using tracking, annotation, and visualization software.

The second section focuses on doing stories with CAR. It covers dealing with the practical challenges of finding and negotiating for data, the principles for cleaning up **dirty data**, building a database when there isn't one, and weaving it altogether to produce better news stories.

In Part 1, Chapter 2 offers tips for searches on the web for datasets, the use of email discussion groups, and downloading data. In recent years, many public databases have been uploaded to the web; this means a journalist doing CAR can get useful data without having to go through the often-painful process of requesting it from officials. This chapter points to some of the most common websites and indices from which to obtain data. It also discusses the columns and rows format of a data table, the challenges with downloading the data, and judging the accuracy of data.

Once a journalist has downloaded data to the computer, he or she is able to do some basic analysis and browsing. Chapter 3 introduces the concepts to dealing with unstructured data: social media, other forms of text, and photos and video.

Chapter 4 introduces spreadsheets, which most journalists agree are the fundamental tool for starting out in computer-assisted analysis. Spreadsheets also are a good way for a journalist to get comfortable with basic math and many of the examples look at how math is applied to cut through the "spin" that politicians or businesses put on numbers.

Chapter 5 deals with the more advanced calculations in spreadsheets and some basic show-how calculations, such as rate and ratio, help focus a story and how data management with a spreadsheet can filter, reshape, visualize, and interpret data. It also introduces the idea of **grouping** records and counting them. The chapter also shows some basic charts and graphs that a spreadsheet can produce to make numbers more understandable.

This chapter serves as a bridge to the Chapter 6, which shows the basics of database managers. It can be a bit more difficult to learn but is the logical next step in data analysis after using spreadsheets. Database managers are frequently used for grouping categories of records and for linking/joining one file or more files (known as tables) of information to another.

Database managers allow you quickly to select columns of information rather than having to "hide" or delete them in Excel. They also filter in or filter out certain kinds of information in rows more easily, can group like records together quickly, and then order the results. In addition, you need a database manager to effectively import and analyze data kept in several tables. Chapter 6 focuses on learning searching and grouping techniques. This chapter uses **Structured Query Language (SQL)** in DB Browser and the "Query by Example" interface provided by the software Microsoft Access to visualize the joining of different tables. While SQL might seem a bit intimidating, it often is a more rapid and intuitive way of examining data for stories. If a journalist knows SQL, the journalist quickly can learn and use any database manager, which is helpful as software rapidly evolves. It also is useful in understanding mapping.

Chapter 7 continues with the application of database managers for linking different tables of information, because that is the form in which some databases are composed (a series of linked tables) or for enterprise stories.

Part 2 deals with the pursuit of the news story and the challenges a journalist faces in doing so. Chapter 8 discusses strategy for getting data that officials are reluctant to distribute, but that may be much more detailed and richer with useful information. Laws that have only begun to catch up with technology and concerns over security and privacy pose barriers to obtaining databases. This chapter examines some of the common obstacles presented by bureaucrats and commercial vendors and advises you on how to get around them. The chapter also looks at methods for finding the right database for the story, requesting the data, and negotiating for data at a reasonable price and within a reasonable time.

Chapter 9 gives you the steps for creating your own databases when a government won't release them or when the database does not exist. This chapter is intended to help student journalists and journalists in small communities whose governments or campuses do not make databases available or do not collect information electronically.

Chapter 10 discusses "dirty data." Dirty data is incomplete or incorrect databases that need to be "cleaned"—that is, completed or corrected. Most, if not all, databases contain errors (just like news reports). A journalist needs to know how to find those errors and either correct them or note them. The cleaning up of dirty data can become complex, but Chapter 10 touches on some of the basic concepts and methods.

In Chapter 11, we talk about strategies for finding and getting started on computer-assisted stories and how *not* to get lost in the abundance of information and possibilities. We look at the steps in doing CAR and how to effectively write a story that uses CAR techniques; review examples and methods to ensure that numbers don't overwhelm a story; and verify that the anecdotal material is representative of the trends and facts discovered while doing data analysis. The chapter also contains advice for how editors and news directors can manage and supervise CAR.

The appendixes to this book are aimed at students and professional, practicing journalists taking the next step after the basics. Both groups need to be aware of the more advanced tools. Among the topics covered are the basics of data visualizations such as mapping and social network analysis.

A Final Thought

CAR is always an adventure with a multitude of possibilities and outcomes. This handbook does not attempt to cover everything in the field of data journalism; instead, it offers enough practical advice to jump-start the hesitant student or journalist into using it for daily, beat, or long-term reporting. One final thought before we get started: a journalist's success in learning CAR depends on that journalist's own efforts no matter how difficult or frustrating it is, or how much CAR may frustrate a journalist.

It's like the old joke:

How many psychiatrists does it take to change a light bulb?

One. But the light bulb has to really want to change.

Chapter Summary

- Journalists need to know how to search for and analyze digital information because it is the way public and business documents are stored, distributed, and kept. It also is a skill that is needed to compete with other news organizations or to get better jobs.
- The three basic tools of CAR are online resources for finding and downloading data, spreadsheets, and data-base managers.
- Once learned, CAR permits a journalist to quickly gather and analyze comprehensive information.
- The best ways to learn the basic software tools are through trial and error, repetition, and intellectually creativity.

Applying CAR

Analyzing city employee salaries for a story on pay equity was reinforced by three lessons I learned at the NICAR boot camp:

- Do your homework.
- Get everything.
- Guarantee a minimum story.

When I approached the personnel directors in cities in the Salt Lake area, I was told that I could have a range of salaries but not the exact earnings of employees. However, I knew from researching my state's open records laws that salaries had to be disclosed. I learned the hard way about getting everything. I had only asked for employee names, salaries, and job tables. I soon realized I also needed information on tenure and the city department in which an employee worked. I ended up going back to the cities. I also had neglected to push for record layouts and code sheets. In this case, I was able to work through the problems.

Third, I learned the value of the minimum story. The most obvious thing—and the easiest story to do—was that female employees were very scarce in top management.

I pursued that angle and found that women who get the same jobs as men earned comparable salaries, but the hang-up was that few women crossed the line from traditional female jobs to traditional male jobs, including top management.

—Edward Carter, *The Deseret News*, Utah

Suggested Exercises

1. Identify three news stories that used data analysis to analyze government databases and won Pulitzer Prizes or international awards. Find explanations on how those stories were done. *Hint*: go the website of IRE, www.ire.org/resourcecenter, for each of these assignments, or the Pulitzer Prize site, www.pulitzer.org/, or gijn.org

2. Identify three news stories that used data analysis on breaking news stories and on follow-up stories. Find explanations on how those stories were done.

3. Decide on which version of Excel you will use for the class.

4. Find the right version the database managers DB Browser SQLite for your computer and download it.

5. Look at the visualization software Arc Online, Tableau, and Data Wrapper.

Part I

Learning Computer-Assisted Reporting Skills

Online Resources

Researching and Finding Data on the Internet

2

Newsday's series revealed that doctors who have been punished for serious or even fatal wrongdoing often continue to work for managed healthcare companies.

The healthcare companies and agencies probably never envisioned their websites being scrutinized in the manner reporter Thomas Maier examined them. From the board-certification website, he found doctors who erroneously claimed board certification in the web listings of managed care companies.

—Richard J. Dalton Jr., formerly of *Newsday*

Maier's reporting, assisted by database expert Dalton, included the use of a large database, numerous interviews, and a successful open-record lawsuit. It was an early example of cross-referencing data on different websites. The concept was straightforward and incorporated one of the basic concepts of a database manager: compare lists of names of doctors who had been reprimanded with the list of names of doctors who were part of a managed care network.

Each of the lists was in a tabular format—columns and rows—which is structured data and most often sought after by journalists when they are online. Unstructured data—text, photos, or videos—is also sought by journalists but it sometimes can be difficult to turn into structured data for analysis (see Chapter 3).

Data journalists now routinely compare data on websites or mine them for data with advanced searches that specifically look for structured data on government, education, or business sites. One effective advanced Google search specifies that the domain name end in .gov and the file type as .xls, indicating that the file is a Microsoft Excel spreadsheet. The search below is looking for government spreadsheets on poverty (see Figure 2.1).

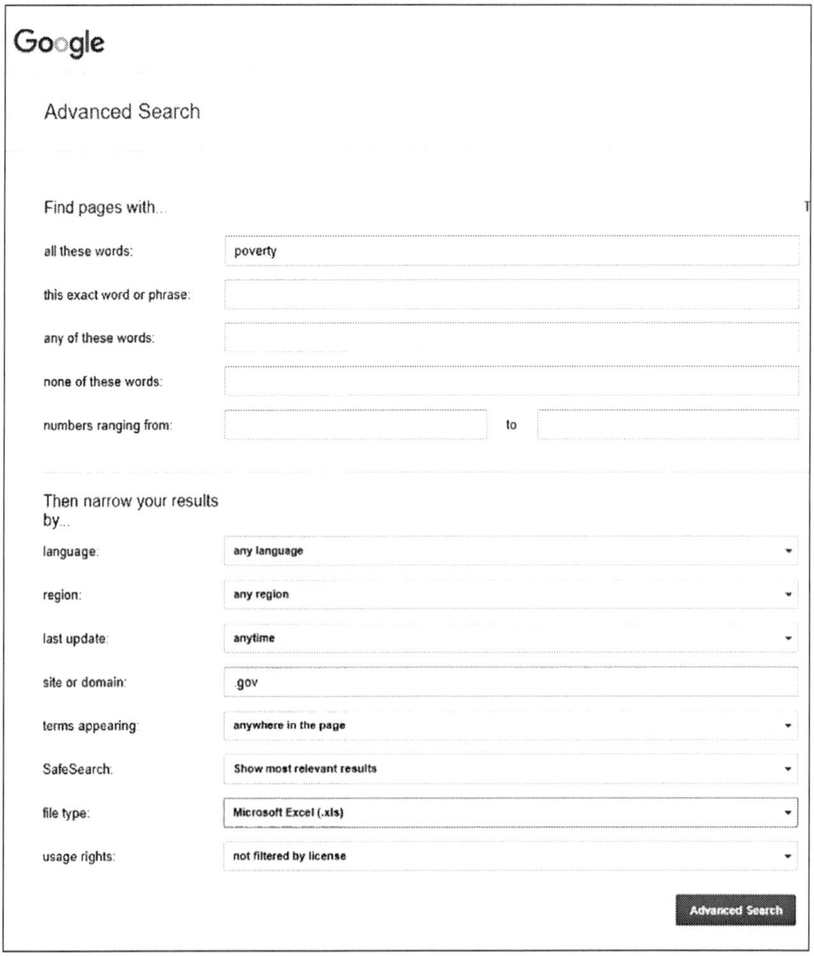

Figure 2.1

In this chapter, we will take a quick look at useful online information and research techniques and then concentrate on finding complete databases and downloading them. We also will address those sites that offer only one or a few records of a website later and talk about web scraping.

BOX 2.1 **Purposes of Online Resources**

Overall, a journalist uses online information for several purposes, including:

- *Research.* A journalist can go to the internet to find databases by searching through discussion groups, books, news stories, academic papers, government reports, and other documents.
- *Interviews.* Online reporting allows a journalist to widen the inquiry and get more information about a database by searching for people involved in or knowledgeable about the database, such as experts, victims, witnesses, and participants. Or journalists can crowd-source for interviewees by sending out a general call for help on a story or for the public to contribute data or data analysis.
- *Database gathering.* A journalist can download an entire dataset to his or her own computer especially when the data comes in different files for different time periods or when only one record or a small group of records can be accessed at a time on the website.
- *Data analysis.* When journalists find a particular database that could be useful, they can not only use a spreadsheet or database manager on their own computers or they can access an analysis program on the server where the database is located.

Finding Data

Before you use a database, you first have to find it. And the one you want to find first is a database that is structured, organized in **columns** and **rows**, and preferably is in a **spreadsheet** format, xls, or **comma separated value (CSV)** format or fixed (columns) because those formats are the easiest to open in or import into a spreadsheet or database manager.

Reporters still do much of their basic analysis working with columns and rows of data, often in a Google Sheet or Microsoft Excel spreadsheet or in a database manager that uses Structured Query Language such the free DB Browser that works on PCs and Macs or Microsoft Access that works only on PCs. Columns and rows allow reporters to sort and summarize data easily in what Richard Mullins, a longtime practitioner, liked to call the "two-dimensional world"—that is, a world reduced to a flat screen of vertical and horizontal information.

On newsrooms websites, we find pages and pages of columns and rows, or what is known as **tabular** information. You may find charts of names and numbers about such topics as census studies, budgets, and taxes. In the business pages, you will see columns and rows detailing stocks, bonds, and mutual funds. In the sports pages, you constantly find the statistics of teams and athletes presented in tabular data form.

Columns are categories of information, and each row (also known as a **record**) has information for each category. On paper and in the often-used **Portable Document Format** (PDF), columns and rows are "petrified" information. That is, the records are static and can't be sorted, filtered, or have calculations performed on them.

But convert those records into one of the formats mentioned above and import those records into a spreadsheet or a database manager, and it suddenly becomes easy to search, sort, and filter them in more meaningful ways. With both a spreadsheet and a database manager, you can change the order of the columns and rows, and you can group categories of data and total it or perform other calculations on it. With a database manager, you can do most of those tasks and, in addition, you can readily join one dataset with another.

For example, journalists frequently want to look at how much public employee salaries are costing taxpayers and who is getting the highest salary. The information regarding people's salaries has at least three categories: name, title, and salary, as shown in Figure 2.2. Each row is a record of each person's information. On paper or in PDF, you have to clumsily rearrange it by hand.

Salaries		
Name	Title	Annual Salary
Josephine Smith	Comptroller	$54,000
Juan Hinojosa	City Manager	$72,000
James Brown	Purchasing Agent	$44,000
Joan Bertrand	Parks Director	$48,000

Figure 2.2

In a spreadsheet, you can sort such a list. In Figure 2.3, we sort the dataset based on salaries from high to low.

	A	B	C
1	Salaries		
2	Name	Title	Annual Salary
3	Juan Hinojosa	City Manager	$72,000
4	Josephine Smith	Comptroller	$54,000
5	Joan Bertrand	Parks Director	$48,000
6	James Brown	Purchasing Agent	$44,000

Figure 2.3

Whether there are four rows of names and salaries or 100,000 rows, it doesn't matter to a spreadsheet or a database manager when it comes to sorting. With the same command you can quickly sort from the highest at the top to the lowest at the bottom—or vice versa.

Digital Information and Data on the Internet

But you first have to find and obtain the data. There are several basic ways to do this. You can download data from the web, acquire it on a storage device such as a DVD or flash drive, or build a database yourself. (In this chapter, we will focus on the getting data from the web.)

With the overwhelming amount of information on the web, finding the right data can be time-consuming and frustrating. But if you approach the web with a plan and an understanding of what is possible to find, you will reap rich results.

Using Online Resources

Although some journalists still struggle with the practical use of online resources, most have learned to make use of them for daily stories and long-term projects.

As long ago as the early 1980s, reporters at *American Banker* and *The Kansas City Star* used **LexisNexis**—a fee-based service of news articles and lawsuits—to research backgrounds and find court cases from across the United States to track international con men who caused the collapses of dozens of lending institutions. Using keywords for the con men and banks, the reporters soon identified which states' lending institutions were affected.

In 1991, Mike Berens, a journalist then at *The Columbus Dispatch* in Ohio, used an online news-clipping library in a ground-breaking investigation to create a database that tracked a multistate serial killer.

By selecting and reviewing unsolved murders of women along interstates, Berens recognized a pattern of killings.

Others have used online databases to detail the deaths of persons from radiation poisoning, measure pollution from environmental toxic sites, track increased housing development in landslide- and earthquake-prone areas, or track nonprofit organization spending. Online forums and social media have helped reporters gather information on terrorist bombings, mass shootings, and city riots.

What Online Resources to Use

One way to research better online is to think of it in two major forms as suggested by the "Investigative Reporter's Handbook": 1) traditional secondary resources, such as the sometimes costly archives of newspapers, academic papers, and business and court records; and 2) primary resources, such as government databases, documents, social media, and discussion groups that cost little or nothing.

The next challenge is to know whether you can trust what you find. You have to verify and cross-reference whatever you find in the online world. You need to determine what websites are credible and who created them. As noted earlier, websites that have addresses ending in ".gov" are created by government agencies and consequently are as reliable as any government information. Others are run by nonprofit groups, some nonpartisan and some advocating for a cause and a web address ending in org. Still others are run by businesses or individuals or individuals, often using government databases and may end in .com. or .net.

As a good journalist, you need to accurately identify the source of the data, do interviews, and compare the information you find with data from other sources that support or contradict information in the database.

Given the rise in "fake news," there are a number of sites that check the veracity of a site's information: Politifact.com, Snopes.com, and Factcheck.org are just a few. But often a journalist has to do the work, especially on a local level, and there are a number of guides to help on that, such as at the Poynter Institute for Media Studies that has fact-checking project where they offer tips at www.poynter.org/tags/fact-checking-tips.

Digital Library Researchers and Journalists

A library researcher is key person for a journalist working online. Professional researchers know where information is stored and how to find it with the right tools. A professional researcher can serve as a guide, providing invaluable advice and knowledge, helping with complex searches, and pointing the journalist to the right resources.

A great example of such an adept researcher is Paul Myers, who works at the British Broadcasting Corporation in London. Myers freely shares his techniques at his website researchclinic.net. Another notable researcher is Margot Williams, who has worked at *The Washington Post*, *The New York Times*, National Public Radio, and The Intercept. Williams often shares her methods in tip sheets that she distributes at journalism conferences.

But journalists need to learn the basics of going into the digital library stacks without help. This is the same principle as learning to use spreadsheets and database managers instead of relying on someone else to do all of your data analysis.

Newsroom Databases

Digital collections of news articles can be extremely valuable in finding databases that have proven useful. There are several commercial services—such as LexisNexis or NewsBank—that provide this kind of resource. Library researchers are skilled in the searching of newspaper archives, and a good journalist never starts a story without checking the archives—also known as "the clips." The service is often free for university faculty and students, but the charges can be significant for private individuals and newsrooms.

Discussion Groups and Social Media

Online discussion groups and social media, such as **listservs**, **Google Groups**, Facebook, or LinkedIn are also constant sources for finding good databases. In some cases, dating websites can especially helpful for backgrounding individuals.

You can join discussion groups or forums in which journalists and programmers discuss data problems and issues. A further advantage of these discussion groups is that you can ask a question of hundreds or thousands of persons at one time. You also can search the archives of these discussion groups to see what has been said.

One long-running listserv to join if you are a journalist or journalism student is the listserv of the National Institute for Computer-Assisted Reporting (NICAR). You can subscribe for free at www.ire.org/resource-center/listservs/subscribe-nicar-l/.

Figure 2.4 lists a selection of just a few discussions.

Patrick, Tim (3)	Inbox	[NICAR-L] Converting hh:mm:ss to ss in Excel - Thanks - that worked perfectly. For anyone looking for the solution worked out mo
Seamus Tuohy	Inbox	[NICAR-L] Hiring: Information Security Technologist at HRW - Hey Everyone, The Information Security team at Human Rights Wa
Dwight Hines	Inbox	[NICAR-L] Third-party transcription services? - India. Best quality checks, quick, all via net, competitive. Google to get list. Dwight
Madolyn Smith	Inbox	[NICAR-L] New resource for the data journalism community from the European Journalism C... - Hi Nicarians, I thought I'd let y
Jennifer Erie (7)	Inbox	[NICAR-L] data journalism etiquette - Thanks for the input! On Thu, May 17, 2018 at 8 25 PM, David Collins wrote: > The practice o
TRAC, David (3)	Inbox	[NICAR-L] ICE Deportations Only Half Levels of Five Years Ago - 'While removals through Secure Communities have recently rec
Jim Feeley	Inbox	[NICAR-L] fwd: Storyful uses tool to monitor what reporters watch - From The Guardian. News to me, but perhaps not to you all

Figure 2.4

Using Boolean Logic to Search the Internet

Without some training and a search strategy, journalists can spend a great deal of wasted time bouncing around the web looking for databases. We will cover **Boolean logic** in more detail later because that logic is the way to methodically search databases and create subsets of databases. But every journalist should know the power and impact of three Boolean words—"and," "or," and "not"—when used in searches. It is not only a **search tool,** but a basis for selecting and filtering records in spreadsheets and database managers.

For example, if you are looking for information on dogs *and* fleas, you will get only information that involves both. If you type that you are looking for information on dogs *or* fleas, you will get a great deal more information because your search results will include information just about dogs, just about fleas, and about both dogs and fleas. If you type that you are looking for information about dogs and *not* fleas, then you will get information about dogs not involving fleas.

Many search engines, such as Google.com automatically choose whether to use *and* or *or* without guidance from you. You can getter a better understanding of Boolean logic by reading the side notes in a Google advanced search page. So, as *The Wall Street Journal* investigative reporter and expert **searcher** Tom McGinty suggests, you should always read each search engine's tips. Google has many search tips and one set can be found at https://support.google.com/websearch/answer/2466433.

Downloading Databases

But back to tabular data. There are now ways to shortcut your searches by going to the portals that collate, or index, free government databases. These portals may access international, national, regional, or local databases.

In the United States, sites such as Data.gov offer links to portals around the world at www.data.gov/open-gov/ to government databases that can be downloaded or analyzed quickly with the methods of spreadsheets and database managers. You can also do some basic analysis with the tools on the site—such as filtering and mapping—before deciding whether to download the data. In fact, working with data on that kind of site can be good tutorial in basic data analysis, such as this one on police arrests in Urbana, Illinois in Figure 2.5. Like many government agencies, Urbana uses the government-funded software Socrata, but others use a free version called CKAN. In either version, you can actually do data analysis on the site itself.

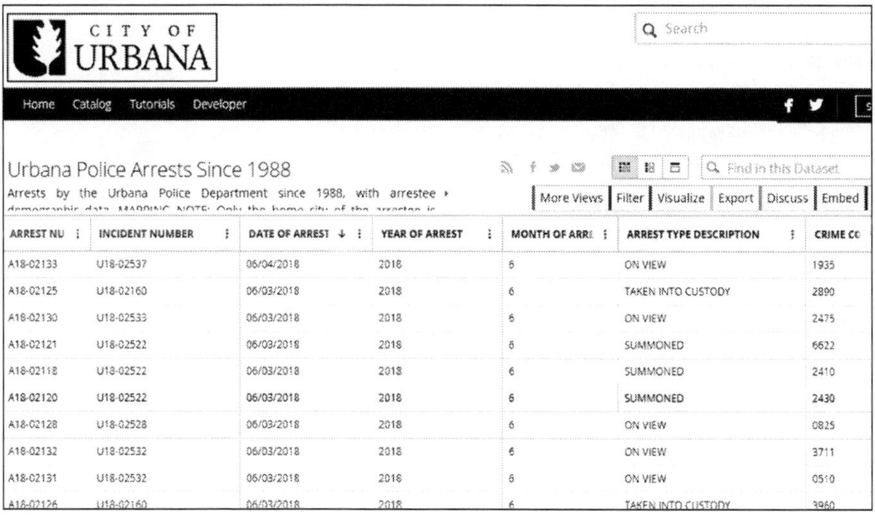

Figure 2.5

Many government agencies throughout the world also have sections of their websites devoted to statistics and data, such as the United Nations' data explorer site at http://data.un.org/Explorer.aspx. The U.S. government has additional gateways to data on both the U.S. and non-U.S. countries at sites such as at the U.S. Census Bureau, www.census.gov/ which you will see later in this chapter. No online portal or index is necessarily complete, but it is a valuable place to start.

BOX 2.2 Different File Types

Tabular databases from the web can come in many forms, most of which can be imported with relative ease into a spreadsheet or a database manager. For example, the U.S. Census Bureau offers files in several formats.

Here is a short list of the common file formats used in databases:

- *Excel or database files.* These files are often listed with .xls or .db as the file extension name as shown before.
- *Delimited files.* These have punctuation marks—commas, semicolons, tabs—between each column of information, often have file extensions of .csv, and spreadsheets and database managers can usually open them easily.
- *Text or fixed format files.* These have the data evenly lined up in straight columns; the file names often have the extension .txt. These files can be imported into a spreadsheet through its import "wizard." Or you can copy parts of data on screen and paste it directly into a spreadsheet.
- *HTML files.* These are tables that have extensions of .html or .php and that often can be read and opened automatically by a spreadsheet. You also can download a file or copy and paste it quickly into a spreadsheet or use a simple web scraper.
- *Portable document files or PDF files.* These are files made for printouts, or otherwise reviewing a static presentation of data, and not for data analysis. They used to be the bane of CAR journalists, but there is now software to convert many of them into spreadsheet format such PDF Acrobat, Cometdocs.com, or tabula. However, if the PDF has been scanned a journalist may be facing a serious challenge in converting the PDF.

Downloading Different Files

Let's do several kinds of downloads and open them in Excel. The first download is from the World Health Organization's statistics site of an Excel worksheet of healthy life expectancy in countries around the world. Here is the site that allows you to download the data (see Figure 2.6).

Healthy life expectancy (HALE)
Data by country
Also available:

— Data by WHO region

filter table | reset table   Download filtered data as: CSV table | XML (simple) | JSC
Last updated: 2018-04-06   Download complete data set as: CSV table | Excel | CSV

	Healthy life expectancy (HALE) at birth (years)[f]														
	Both sexes					Male					Female				
Country	2016	2015	2010	2005	2000	2016	2015	2010	2005	2000	2016	2015	2010	2005	2000
Afghanistan	53.0	53.2	51.6	49.6	46.9	52.1	52.6	50.9	49.1	46.2	54.1	54.1	52.3	50.2	47.7
Albania	68.1	67.8	66.4	65.4	64.9	66.7	66.5	64.7	64.0	62.9	69.6	69.3	68.2	67.0	67.2
Algeria	65.5	65.3	64.5	62.8	60.7	65.4	65.2	64.4	62.7	60.3	65.6	65.4	64.6	63.0	61.2
Angola	55.8	55.3	51.8	46.7	41.9	53.8	53.3	49.9	44.9	40.1	57.7	57.3	53.7	48.4	43.7
Antigua and Barbuda	67.0	66.9	66.5	65.4	64.6	65.2	65.1	64.8	64.0	62.5	68.8	68.6	68.1	66.9	66.6
Argentina	68.4	68.2	67.3	66.7	65.7	65.9	65.7	64.9	64.2	63.0	70.7	70.5	69.7	69.3	68.4
Armenia	66.3	66.0	65.2	64.7	63.8	63.6	63.3	61.7	61.8	61.3	68.7	68.5	68.4	67.4	66.1
Australia	73.0	72.7	72.2	71.4	70.3	71.8	71.5	70.9	69.9	68.5	74.1	73.9	73.5	72.9	72.0

Figure 2.6

By clicking on the Excel or CSV tab at the top of the screen, it automatically downloads into Excel as in Figure 2.7. You need only save it to the folder in which you wish to keep it on your computer; then you can begin your analysis. (You may get a few more columns than show on the website, but it's the same data.)

Another kind of file sometimes comes in fixed format, although usually it is an older file when websites did offer Excel or CSV.

For this example, we downloaded an older fixed format file from the web that is a list of special taxing districts by state in the U.S. These generally have an extension of .txt. When we download and open it with notepad software in Figure 2.8 we see how the columns are lined up.

	A	B	C	D	E	F	G
1		Healthy life expectancy	Healthy life expectancy	Healthy life expectancy	Healthy life expectancy	Healthy life expectancy	Healthy life expectancy
2		Both sexes	Both sexes	Both sexes	Both sexes	Both sexes	Male
3	Country	2016	2015	2010	2005	2000	2016
4	Afghanistan	53	53.2	51.6	49.6	46.9	52.1
5	Albania	68.1	67.8	66.4	65.4	64.9	66.7
6	Algeria	65.5	65.3	64.5	62.8	60.7	65.4
7	Angola	55.8	55.3	51.8	46.7	41.9	53.8
8	Antigua and Barbuda	67	66.9	66.5	65.4	64.6	65.2
9	Argentina	68.4	68.2	67.3	66.7	65.7	65.9
10	Armenia	66.3	66	65.2	64.7	63.8	63.6
11	Australia	73	72.7	72.2	71.4	70.3	71.8
12	Austria	72.4	72.1	71.4	70.6	69.5	70.9
13	Azerbaijan	64.9	64.6	63.4	61.5	59.6	62.8
14	Bahamas	66.8	66.7	66.4	65.1	63.7	64.7
15	Bahrain	68.1	67.7	66.3	64.5	63	68.3
16	Bangladesh	63.3	62.8	60.7	58.6	56.5	62.6
17	Barbados	67	66.8	66.2	65.8	65.1	65.4
18	Belarus	65.5	65.2	62.3	60.8	60.8	61.4
19	Belgium	71.6	71.4	70.8	69.9	68.9	70.2

Figure 2.7

2007gid_counties - Notepad

File Edit Format View Help

```
01100100100000AUTAUGA          COUNTY          CHAIRMAN             134 NORTH COU
01100700700000BUTLER           COUNTY          CHAIRMAN             P.O. BOX 756
01101101100000CHILTON          COUNTY          CHAIRMAN             P.O. BOX 1948
01101801800000CONECUH          COUNTY          CHAIRMAN             P.O. BOX 347
01102302300000DALE             COUNTY          PROBATE JUDGE        202 HWY. 123
01103603600000JACKSON          COUNTY          CHAIRMAN             102 E. LAUREL
01104004000000LAWRENCE         COUNTY          CHAIRMAN             750 MAIN STRE
01104704700000MARION           COUNTY          CHAIRMAN             PO BOX 460
01105405400000PICKENS          COUNTY          CHAIRMAN             P.O. BOX 460
01106506500000WASHINGTON       COUNTY          PROBATE JUDGE        P.O. BOX 146
```

Figure 2.8

In looking at that data we know we are going to need guidelines on how to slice it into columns, and that is what a **record layout** will do. We will talk about record layouts in later chapters, but this is a good time to see why it is so important to get a layout such as the one in Figure 2.9.

FILE LAYOUT FOR 2007gid_counties.txt

2007 Governments Integrated Directory - Counties

Field Name	Positions	Start Position	Length	Characteristic
State	01-02	01	2	Governments ID - State code 01 - Alabama thru 51 - Wyoming
Type	03-03	03	1	Governments ID - Type of Government code Always '1' (indicates "county government")
County	04-06	04	3	Governments ID - County code Numeric
Unit	07-09	07	3	Governments ID - Unit code Numeric
Supplement	10-12	10	3	Governments ID - Supplement code Always '000' (records are independent governn
Sub Code	13-14	13	2	Governments ID - Sub code Always '00' (records are independent governm
Government Name	15-78	15	64	Name of governmental unit

Figure 2.9

The record layout file shows what columns the information goes in and how wide the columns are. They sometimes include translations of codes and the type of data—text, numeric, or date.

You can see the record layout tells you how many spaces the data gets in each column, much like a crossword puzzle. When you import fixed format data into a spreadsheet such as Excel, this information is critical to having an accurate download and to importing the data into a spreadsheet.

Now comes the tricky part: opening this file with Excel. When we click on "Open" under "File," a "Wizard" screen appears as in Figure 2.10. The Wizard notes whether the text is in fixed format or includes delimiters, such as commas.

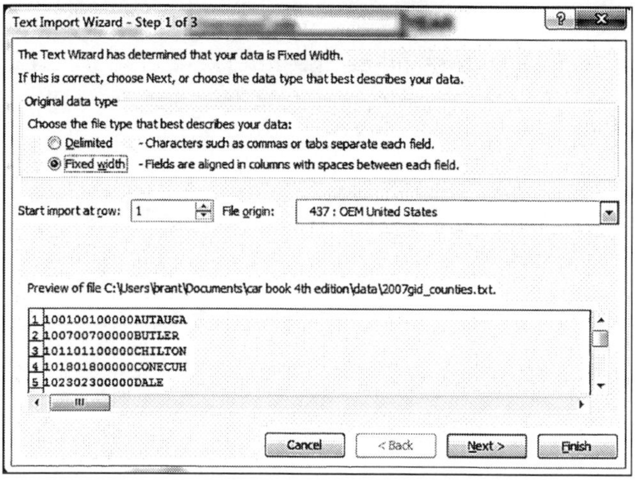

Figure 2.10

In this case, we choose "Fixed Width" because it is a text file in which the columns (also called "**Fields**") are already left justified and should have spaces in between. When we click "Next," we find that we now can draw the lines in the data to establish columns and can also delete or move the lines as we wish.

Sometimes Excel guesses the right places to put the lines, but in the beginning part of this data it does not. Therefore, it is up to us to create lines at the correct spaces according to the file record layout which notes that "state" is the first two spaces, "type of government" is the third space, "county" is the next three spaces and so on as in Figure 2.11.

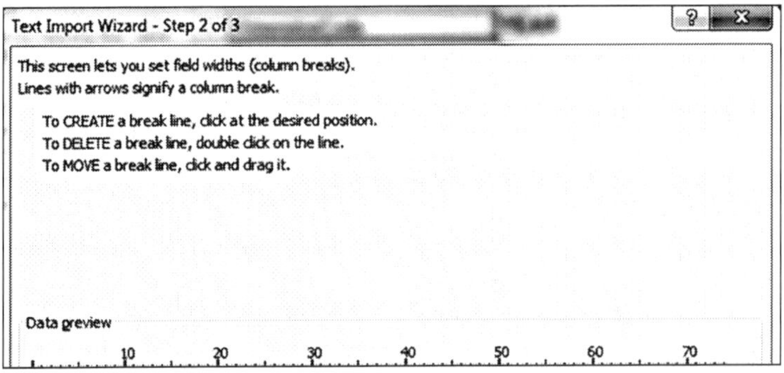

Figure 2.11

After drawing the proper lines in the data, according to the record layout, we hit "Next" and see that the Wizard now allows us to determine the correct data types for each column as in Figure 2.12. In this case, we will use whatever the program suggests by accepting "General." (We will talk about data types in later chapters.)

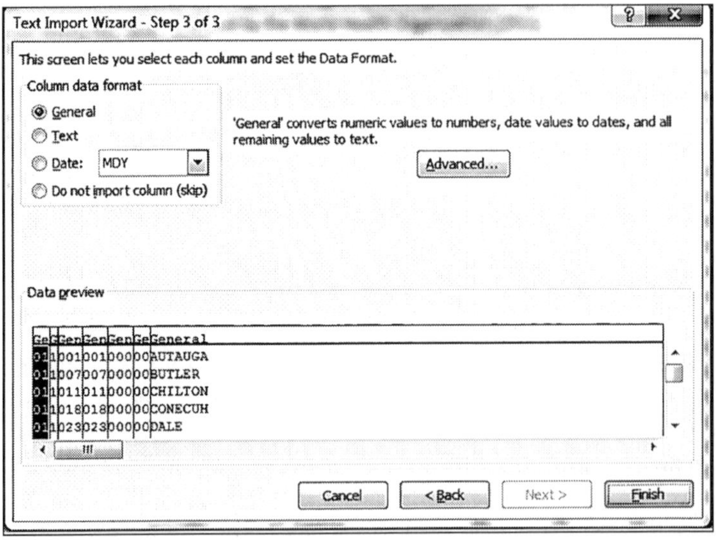

Figure 2.12

When we click "Finish," we will have the data in the worksheet and be ready for analysis as in Figure 2.13. Upon completing this step, you should immediately save the file as an Excel file.

A	B	C	D	E	F	G	H	I	J	K	L	M	N
1	1	1	1	0	0	AUTAUGA	COUNTY	CHAIRMAN	134 NORTH COURT S	PRATTVILLE		AL	36067
1	1	7	7	0	0	BUTLER	COUNTY	CHAIRMAN	P.O. BOX 756	GREENVILLE		AL	36037
1	1	11	11	0	0	CHILTON	COUNTY	CHAIRMAN	P.O. BOX 1948	CLANTON		AL	35046
1	1	18	18	0	0	CONECUH	COUNTY	CHAIRMAN	P.O. BOX 347	EVERGREEN		AL	36401
1	1	23	23	0	0	DALE	COUNTY	PROBATE JUDGE	202 HWY. 123 SOUTH	OZARK		AL	36360
1	1	36	36	0	0	JACKSON	COUNTY	CHAIRMAN	102 E. LAUREL STREE	SCOTTSBORO		AL	35768
1	1	40	40	0	0	LAWRENCE	COUNTY	CHAIRMAN	750 MAIN STREET	MOULTON		AL	35650
1	1	47	47	0	0	MARION	COUNTY	CHAIRMAN	PO BOX 460	HAMILTON		AL	35570
1	1	54	54	0	0	PICKENS	COUNTY	CHAIRMAN	P.O. BOX 460	CARROLLTON		AL	35447
1	1	65	65	0	0	WASHINGTON	COUNTY	PROBATE JUDGE	P.O. BOX 146	CHATOM		AL	36518
1	1	31	31	0	0	GENEVA	COUNTY	COMMISSION, CHAIRMAN/PROB	P.O. BOX 430	GENEVA		AL	36340
3	1	8	8	0	0	MOHAVE	COUNTY	SUPERVISOR, CHAIR	401 SPRING STREET	KINGMAN		AZ	86401
1	1	4	4	0	0	BIBB	COUNTY	COMMISSIONER, CHAIR	157 SW DAVIDSON D	CENTREVILLE		AL	35042
5	1	9	9	0	0	EL DORADO	COUNTY	SUPERVISOR, CHAIR	330 FAIR LANE	PLACERVILLE		CA	95667
5	1	11	11	0	0	GLENN	COUNTY	SUPERVISOR, CHAIR	525 WEST SYCAMORI	WILLOWS		CA	95988
5	1	32	32	0	0	PLUMAS	COUNTY	SUPERVISOR, CHAIR	520 MAIN STREET, RC	QUINCY		CA	95971
5	1	35	35	0	0	SAN BENITO	COUNTY	SUPERVISOR, CHAIR	481 FOURTH STREET	HOLLISTER		CA	95023
5	1	43	42	0	0	SANTA CLARA	COUNTY	COUNTY EXECUTIVE OFFICER	70 W HEDDING, 10TH	SAN JOSE		CA	95110
5	1	58	57	0	0	YUBA	COUNTY	SUPERVISOR, CHAIRMAN	215 5TH STREET	MARYSVILLE		CA	95901
21	1	11	10	0	0	FREDERICK	COUNTY	EXECUTIVE DIRECTOR	12 E. CHURCH STREET	FREDERICK		MD	21701
21	1	12	11	0	0	GARRETT	COUNTY	COMMISSIONER, CHAIRMAN	203 SOUTH FOURTH S	OAKLAND		MD	21550
31	1	1	1	0	0	ATLANTIC	COUNTY	COUNTY EXECUTIVE	1333 ATLANTIC AVE.	ATLANTIC CITY		NJ	8401
31	1	18	18	0	0	SOMERSET	COUNTY	FREEHOLDER DIRECTOR	20 GROVE STREET	SOMERVILLE		NJ	8876
44	1	8	8	0	0	AUSTIN	COUNTY	COUNTY JUDGE	ONE EAST MAIN STRI	BELLVILLE		TX	77418
44	1	56	56	0	0	DALLAM	COUNTY	COUNTY JUDGE	P.O. BOX 9395	DALHART		TX	79022
44	1	79	79	0	0	FORT BEND	COUNTY	COUNTY JUDGE	301 JACKSON STREET	RICHMOND		TX	77469

Figure 2.13

Next, we will try downloading delimited files of the same information. The standard delimited file is the "CSV" file, and most CSV files are as easy to download into Excel as Excel files. For example, the CSV file on cases of tuberculosis around the world opens automatically in Excel when you download it—that is, as long as you have Excel on your computer. We click on the file on the web as in Figure 2.14.

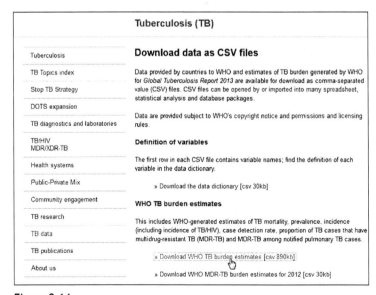

Figure 2.14

When downloaded the data goes directly into Excel. All you have to do is save it as an Excel file and do your analysis (see Figure 2.15).

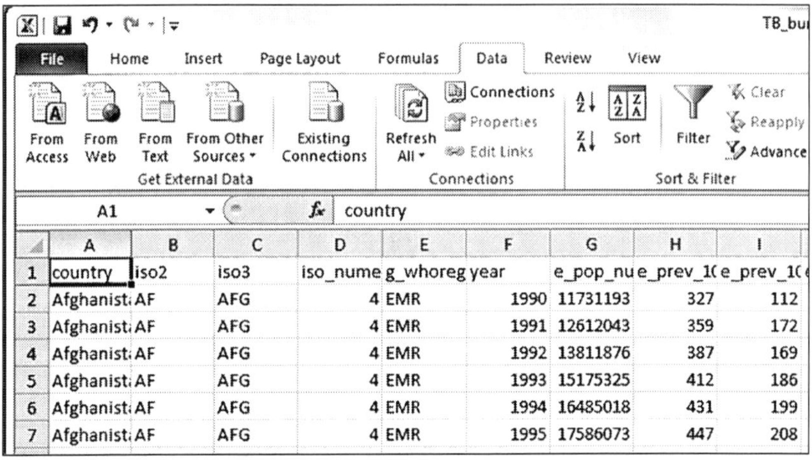

Figure 2.15

Sometimes, however, a file will say it is a CSV file, but the delimiters could be a semicolon or a "tab" or some other character. For example, consider the database on gun dealers in the United States shown in Figure 2.16. As you import it, you can see it much like a fixed format file except using tabs. So changing the "delimiter" to tab arranges the data properly.

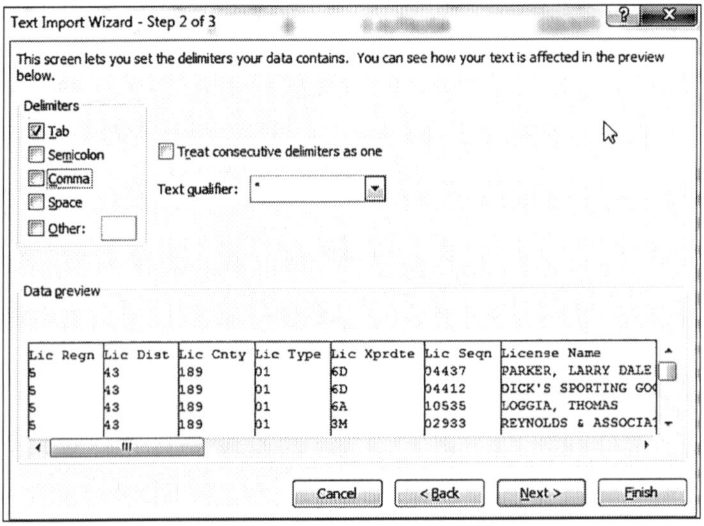

Figure 2.16

When dealing with PDF files, there are now some quick solutions. For example, a city posts the salaries and other information on its website, but only in PDF format as in Figure 2.17.

Name	Title	Group	Moving Expenses	Vehicle Allowance	Clothing Allowance	Other Earnings	Earnings	Health Insurance
ALLEN, AARON S	ST MW II-01	AFSCME			$ 566.00	$ 833.13	$ 78,343.13	$ 8,986.64
ANDERSON, MIKE D	SS MW II-01	AFSCME			$ 566.00	$ 833.13	$ 61,433.65	$ 12,655.52
BARNES, SARAH E	TELECOM I-06	AFSCME				$ 833.13	$ 39,206.95	$ 6,361.32
BARR, AMELIA E	TELECOM I-21	AFSCME				$ 833.13	$ 66,312.88	$ 10,452.24
BEASLEY, MENDY J	TELECOM I-22	AFSCME				$ 833.13	$ 67,299.79	$ 7,319.44
BECKMAN, STEPHEN	CONC MWII-01	AFSCME			$ 566.00	$ 833.13	$ 82,960.16	$ 12,329.36
BEHNEKE, WANDA Y	CS REP-04	AFSCME				$ 833.13	$ 53,084.72	$ 2,400.00
BELLMORE, DAVID P	TELECOM I-18	AFSCME				$ 833.13	$ 74,226.18	$ 7,318.88
BENNETT, KATHRYN	POL S REP-04	AFSCME					$ 12,738.63	$ 2,441.60
BIDWELL, PAULA J	POLINFRES-08	AFSCME			$ 418.00	$ 833.13	$ 55,145.78	$ 7,318.64
BIGHAM, DENNIS	ST MW II-03	AFSCME			$ 566.00	$ 833.13	$ 81,502.81	$ 12,713.68
BRAUER, LAURIE	TELECOM I-06	AFSCME					$ 11,650.96	$ 600.00
BRAZELTON, DEANNE L	TELECOM I-05	AFSCME				$ 833.13	$ 69,705.97	$ 7,318.88
BREWER, SETH M	AC CLK II-03	AFSCME				$ 833.13	$ 53,160.13	$ 12,719.20

Figure 2.17

An online service that many journalists use is CometDocs.com. Its basic service is free. You upload your PDF file to CometDocs interface—in this case it is called total compensation—and drag it to the bottom window and choose to convert it to Excel by choosing Excel in the lower window, as in Figure 2.17.

As you can see in Figures 2.18 and 2.19, you can download data in several formats. You might download the text file because you want to filter out some kinds of records before importing the data into Excel or eventually importing it into some other kind of analytical software. CometDocs also can email the file to you.

Figure 2.18a

Figure 2.18b

In Figure 2.19, it downloads as Excel.

	A	B	C
1			
2			
3	City of Champaign Employee Compensation Report		
4			
5	Earned		
6			Total
7	Name	Title	Compensation
8	ALLEN, AARON S	ST MW II-01	$102,151.41
9	ANDERSON, MIKE D	SS MW II-01	$85,173.11
10	BARNES, SARAH E	TELECOM I-06	$52,869.22
11	BARR, AMELIA E	TELECOM I-21	$89,244.98
12	BEASLEY, MENDY J	TELECOM I-22	$87,617.06
13	BECKMAN, STEPHEN	CONC MWII-01	$110,796.33
14	BEHNEKE, WANDA Y	CS REP-04	$66,194.19
15	BELLMORE, DAVID P	TELECOM I-18	$95,779.86
16	BENNETT, KATHRYN	POL S REP-04	$17,660.44
17	BIDWELL, PAULA J	POLINFRES-08	$73,023.18
18	BIGHAM, DENNIS	ST MW II-03	$109,295.95

Figure 2.19

There always is the potential of problems in downloading databases: sometimes the delimiter is misidentified; sometimes there are hidden marks or characters in the data. But if you go slowly and make sure to closely examine the data, you can usually figure out the problem yourself. Once you do that, you are ready do data analysis in pursuit of the good story.

Web Scraping

There are other times you run into data on the web that requires you to look at one record or one part of a dataset at a time. We will not get into all the complexities of web scraping—and it can get complex—but we want to just point out that this is becoming a much more common way of finding and downloading data that is put in a convenient format of csv or xls.

An example of a basic tool to add to a web **browser** for Google Chrome is "Scraper," which you can get for free from the Google App store as in Figure 2.20.

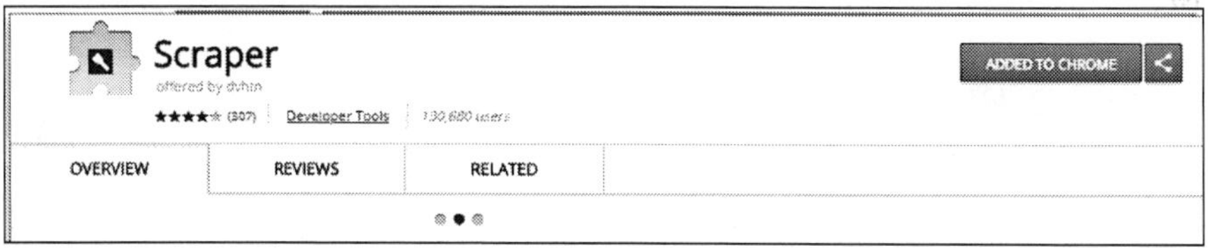

Figure 2.20

A scraper comes in handy when you see a dataset on the web, such as at the waiting list for organ transplants by state—https://optn.transplant.hrsa.gov/data/view-data-reports/national-data/#—as in Figure 2.21.

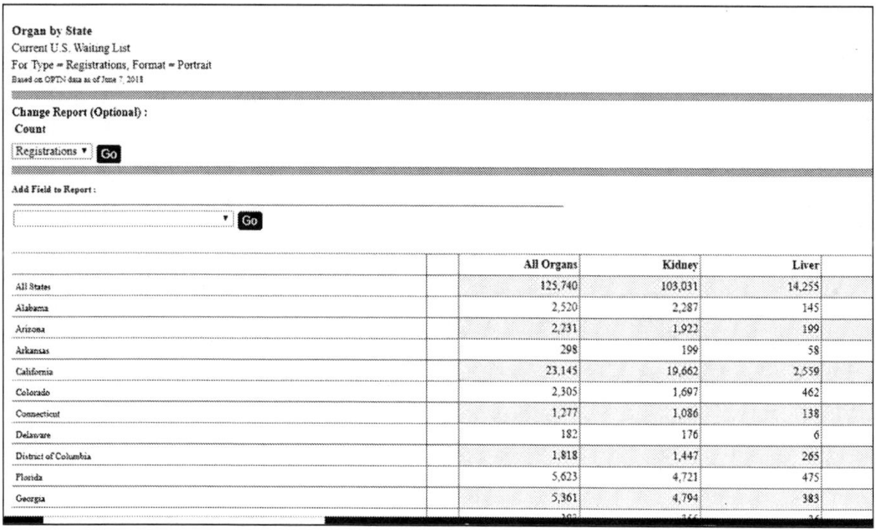

Organ by State
Current U.S. Waiting List
For Type = Registrations, Format = Portrait
Based on OPTN data as of June 7, 2011

Change Report (Optional) :
Count
Registrations ▾ Go

Add Field to Report :
▾ Go

	All Organs	Kidney	Liver
All States	125,740	103,031	14,255
Alabama	2,520	2,287	145
Arizona	2,231	1,922	199
Arkansas	298	199	58
California	23,145	19,662	2,559
Colorado	2,305	1,697	462
Connecticut	1,277	1,086	138
Delaware	182	176	6
District of Columbia	1,818	1,447	265
Florida	5,623	4,721	475
Georgia	5,361	4,794	383

Figure 2.21

There are no apparent Excel or CSV files to download and it could be a bit of work to copy and paste the tabular information. But once you have added Scraper to your browser you highlight the first row of records as in Figure 2.22.

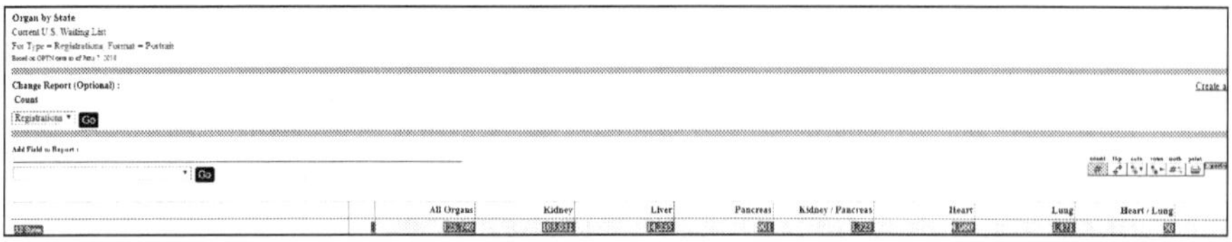

Figure 2.22

If you right click on your mouse, "Scrape similar" comes up as in Figure 2.23.

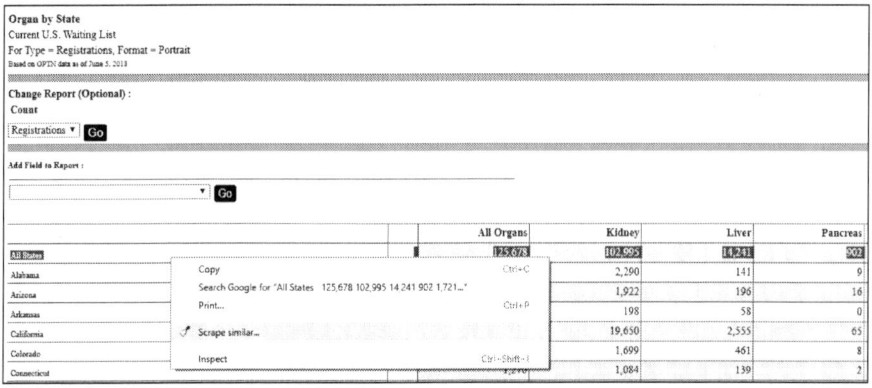

Figure 2.23

The data will all be imported to the tabular file in Figure 2.24.

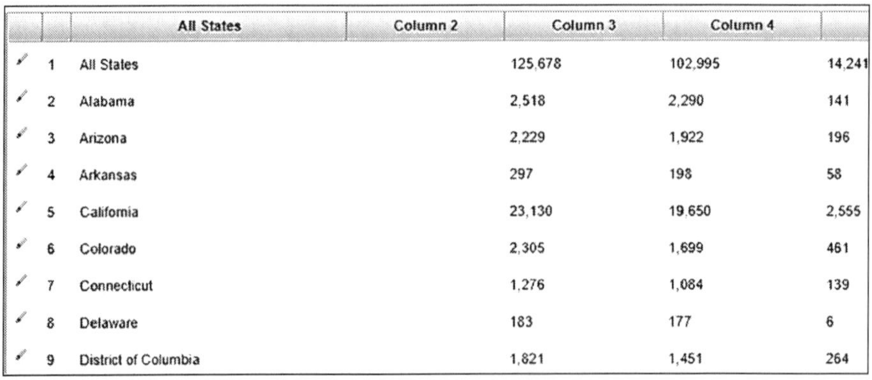

		All States	Column 2	Column 3	Column 4
	1	All States	125,678	102,995	14,241
	2	Alabama	2,518	2,290	141
	3	Arizona	2,229	1,922	196
	4	Arkansas	297	198	58
	5	California	23,130	19,650	2,555
	6	Colorado	2,305	1,699	461
	7	Connecticut	1,276	1,084	139
	8	Delaware	183	177	6
	9	District of Columbia	1,821	1,451	264

Figure 2.24

At the bottom of the file there is an Export to Google Docs button. You click on that and that data ends up in columns and rows as in Figure 2.25. (You will have to put in most of the column headers, but that is not much work at all.)

	A	B	C	D	E	F
1	All States	Column 2	Column 3	Column 4	Column 5	Column 6
2	All States		125,740	103,031	14,255	901
3	Alabama		2,520	2,287	145	9
4	Arizona		2,231	1,922	199	16
5	Arkansas		298	199	58	0
6	California		23,145	19,662	2,559	64
7	Colorado		2,305	1,697	462	8
8	Connecticut		1,277	1,086	138	2
9	Delaware		182	176	6	0
10	District of Colum		1,818	1,447	265	23
11	Florida		5,623	4,721	475	17
12	Georgia		5,361	4,794	383	10
13	Hawaii		383	355	26	0
14	Illinois		4,287	3,534	352	45

Figure 2.25

Scraper and other scraping software can do much more than this, whether it is combining a series of tables or collecting data from a site that only lets you see one record at a time. It takes some work to learn all the nuances, but it opens up another whole level of data downloading.

Chapter Summary

- The internet can be used for several purposes, including obtaining contacts, doing research, and finding and using databases.
- Listservs, forums, newsgroups, and social media are ways to find discussion on specific topics.

- Begin every story by checking electronic news archives and using search engines.
- Indexes are efficient ways to get started on research.
- Many government websites have data that can be downloaded for analysis, and many governments have databases on other countries.
- There are several kinds of database formats, all of which can be imported into spreadsheets and database managers with varying levels of difficulty.
- If a complete database is not available in one of the typical formats, a web scraper allows you to capture and collate the data.

Applying CAR

The Arkansas Democrat-Gazette embarked on a detailed look at nonprofit, private foundations in Arkansas and found an astounding number. Arkansas's 273 private foundations controlled about $1.5 billion in assets and handed out $116 million in one year. And that's for a state that lags economically behind the rest of the nation. Without the foundations, the impoverished Mississippi River Delta would [be] even more desperate.

To understand the foundations' impact, we followed the money and got the 990-PF forms that foundations have to file with the Internal Revenue Service (IRS) and got electronic data from the National Center for Charitable Statistics. But the information goes further. Going online from a desktop computer, we found a large collection of websites devoted to the nonprofit world in general and foundations in particular.

One information gold mine was the Foundation Center in New York. The organization's website and its publications were invaluable. At the Foundation Center's website, you find a foundation's records on gift recipients, foundation officers, and more.

The IRS itself has a plethora of nonprofit related information online, including data files listing all nonprofits. The nonprofit organization Guidestar (www.guidestar.org)

collects and posts the information submitted by most non-profits to the IRS.

Our first story included key statistics on the overall picture of foundations. Our second story focused on the details of the foundation money flowing into the Delta. Our third story looked at the impact of the Walton Family Foundation.

—Jeff Porter, formerly of *The Arkansas
Democrat-Gazette*, now data library
director at the Association for
Healthcare Journalists

Suggested Exercises

1. Find three international websites, three federal government websites, and three state websites that have data.
2. Download data from one of these sites.
3. Import the data into a spreadsheet.
4. Join the NICAR-L listserv and find two other journalism data websites to follow.

Gathering and Analyzing Text and Social Media

3

So we used Project Backlight, which is open source software normally used by librarians. We used it for the journalists. It's simple because it allows you to do faceted search—so, for example, you can facet by the folder structure of the leak, by years, by type of file. There were more complex things—it supports queries in regular expressions, so the more advanced users were able to search for documents with a certain pattern of numbers that, for example, passports use. You could also preview and download the documents.

—Mar Cabra, who worked on the Panama
Papers, which were leaked stories about
offshore companies based on more than
two terabytes of data

One of the most challenging parts of my job is the massive number of documents I have to read, most of which are junk, but hidden in there are some real gems. A PDF reader is just not good enough. I have traditionally used Adobe Acrobat Pro DC, as it has good optical character recognition tools, which index the words on each page, allowing you to do word searches. More recently, I have been trying out a service called Logical, created for law firms to do document discovery work but useful when trying to analyze and annotate piles of documents that I get via Freedom of Information Act requests, which in some cases can run to 18,000 pages. Document Cloud is also a tremendous tool.

—Eric Lipton, *The New York Times*

Over the past decade, journalists have had to become more sophisticated in analyzing documents, email, social media, and other forms of unstructured data. Freedom of information requests can result in tens of thousands of pages of memos and emails that need to be analyzed accurately and speedily. Leaks of millions of confidential documents such as the Panama Papers need to be converted into some kind of structured data to productively search and index documents to find patterns and connections. Social media posts and tweets offer an incredible amount of tips and information when downloaded and analyzed.

Unstructured data—text, audio, photos, or video—also encourages more visualization of large datasets so that patterns and **outliers** can be more rapidly recognized and infographics and interactive presentations presented. The need to deal with unstructured data has also increased library and information scientists and archivists, who also have dealt for many years with the issues of efficiently searching, analyzing, storing, and retrieving unstructured data.

One of the most basic ways journalists realized the power of visualization of unstructured text was when they were introduced to "Word Clouds." The software counts the number of times a word or phrase is repeated in the transcript of a speech or some other document and then represents the amount of repetition by the size of the word in the visualization. Journalists have moved far ahead of this kind of analysis, but it still is useful for a fast look at what the speaker was emphasizing. Generally, you open the Word Cloud software and you can either copy and paste the text of a transcript or import it. As shown in Figure 3.1, we opened the free

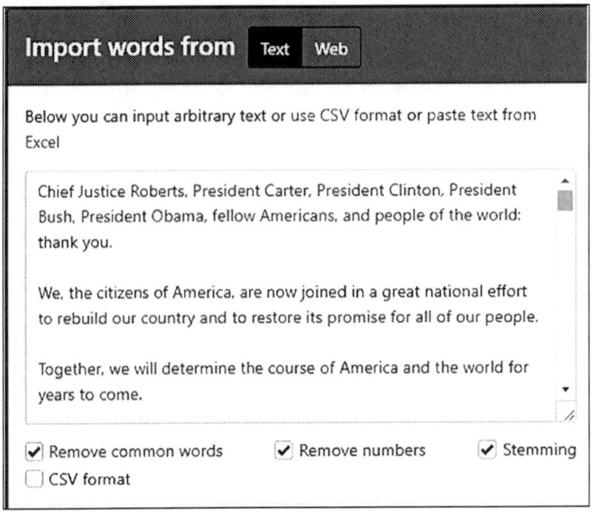

Figure 3.1

software, Word Art, and tapped on "Import" and we copied and pasted the transcript of President Donald Trump's inaugural speech in 2017.

The software counts the words, leaving out common words like "the" and "or" in Trump's speech, as in Figure 3.2.

WORDS						✗ Visualize
🛢 Import ➕ Add — Remove ⬆ Up ⬇ Down					⚙ Options	
Filter	Size	Color	Angle	Font		
America	18	Default	Default	Default	▾	
American	16	Default	Default	Default	▾	
Nation	13	Default	Default	Default	▾	
Country	12	Default	Default	Default	▾	
People	9	Default	Default	Default	▾	
One	9	Default	Default	Default	▾	
Again	9	Default	Default	Default	▾	

Figure 3.2

Then we clicked on "Visualize" and produced the result in Figure 3.3.

Figure 3.3

We did the same for Obama's 2013 speech and produced this visualization in Figure 3.4.

Figure 3.4

Even with this elementary approach, you can compare what each president was emphasizing in the speech, both similarities and differences. Using a word cloud also starts a journalist thinking about analyzing text.

However, that is only one document and journalists often need to deal with many documents at one time, as Cabra and Lipton point out. One of best sites at which journalists can start is DocumentCloud.org, as in Figure 3.5. Created by journalists for journalists, DocumentCloud offers a free subscription to journalists so they can upload documents that be converted into data for analysis and annotation.

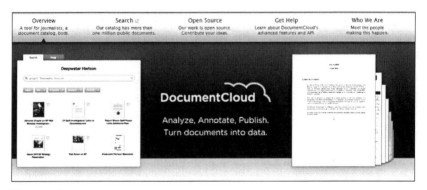

Figure 3.5

DocumentCloud uses the software, Open Calais, provided by Reuters, to convert documents and provide links to related information in other documents and data to better identify people and places and provide more information about them, as stated on the Reuters' Open Calais site in Figure 3.6.

Figure 3.6

BOX 3.1 **Open Calais**

As Reuters explains on its website: "Reuters uses Natural Language Processing and machine learning algorithms. As Reuters says, "For the user, the process is pretty simple. You feed unstructured text into the extraction engine (news articles, blog postings, etc.) to examine your text and locate:

- Entities: (Companies, people, places, products, etc.).
- Relationships: (John Doe works for Acme Corp.).
- Facts: (John Doe is a 42-year old male CFO).
- Events: (Jane Doe was appointed a board member of Acme Corp.).
- Topics: (Story is about M&As in the Pharma industry)."

Journalists have used DocumentCloud to more thoroughly pore through thousands of documents, seeing connections where they might not have seen by just reading through the documents, and to annotate the important part of the documents. Stories have included uncovering faulty medical devices, questionable speeding tickets, political lobbying records, leaked emails from federal officials, nonprofit filings, and national security issues.

Here is an example of the Peoria, IL newspaper using DocumentCloud for entities in a police complaint in Figure 3.7. Under the tab Analyze, you can choose to View Entities or View Timeline.

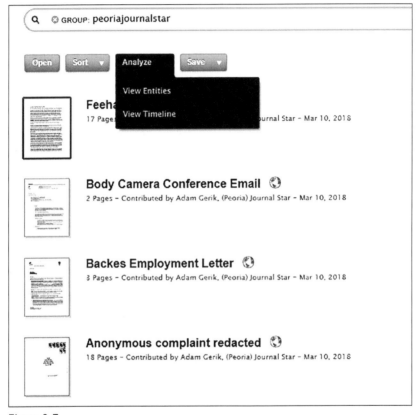

Figure 3.7

You can see the software has plucked out the "entities"—people, organizations (and off the screen are places)—from the complaint document as shown in Figure 3.8.

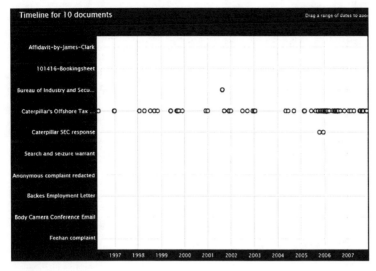

Figure 3.8

And in Figure 3.8 Open Calais has provided a timeline across ten documents that on which a reporter can zoom in for detail. In each case, clicking on the mark can take you back to the original document.

These are a few of the tools in DocumentCloud for dealing with text. Another useful tool is annotating documents, both during reporting and for viewers as an AP reporter did on this Department of Justice advisory letter in Figure 3.9.

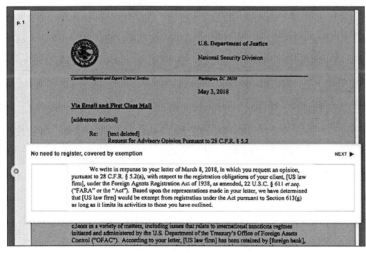

Figure 3.9

Social Media for News Gathering and Analysis

Journalists want to use social media for news gathering and analysis, and simpler tools are being developed. Currently, some of the best tools require coding abilities but there are still non-coding ways to do that within the social media themselves, and with some free applications.

First, however, a reporter needs a checklist. When searching and copying social media into word files, it often can be the last social media site a reporter checks that delivers the important information. A journalist sometimes forgets what a powerful resource social media is for reporting because a journalist has used social media more for communicating with family and friends. In addition, it is good to know some of the basic tips and tools for getting news and background of people, organizations, and places.

BOX 3.2 Kinds of Social Media

Here is a partial list check-list of social media for research on people and organizations. You can add other local or topic specific sites.

- Twitter
- Facebook
- LinkedIn
- Instagram
- Pinterest
- Tumblr
- Reddit
- SnapChat
- Next Door Neighbor
- Tinder and other dating sites

As noted in Chapter 2, often the best place to start with searches on social media sites is with the sites' own guides. Twitter, for example, offers an Advanced Search, as in Figure 3.10 which looks much like Google Advanced Search.

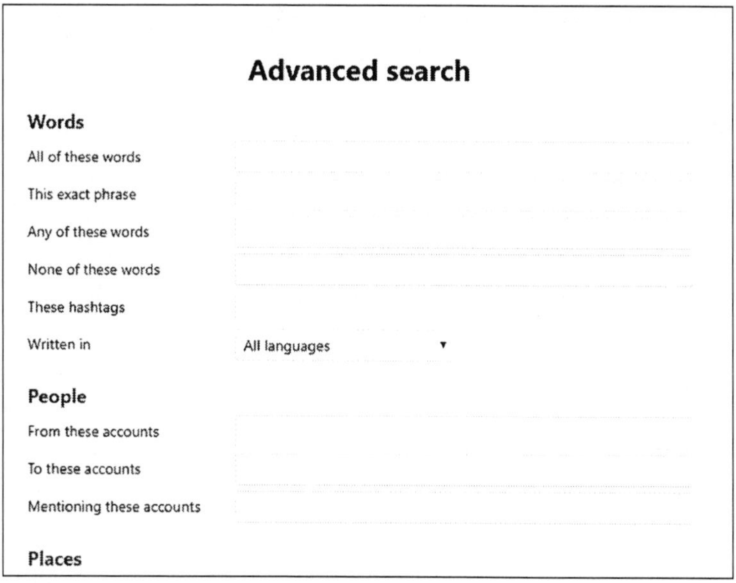

Advanced search

Words

All of these words

This exact phrase

Any of these words

None of these words

These hashtags

Written in   All languages   ▼

People

From these accounts

To these accounts

Mentioning these accounts

Places

Figure 3.10

Facebook, too, has advanced search pages as seen in Figure 3.11, which journalists sometimes neglect to use.

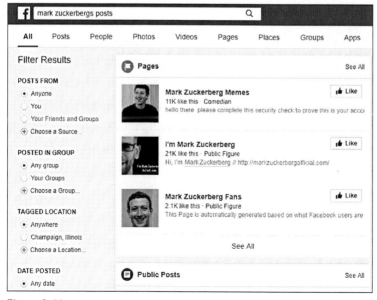

Figure 3.11

The LinkedIn search tool can run searches based on name, company, schools, groups, and location as in Figure 3.12.

All people filters

First name	Company	Connections
Last name	School	1st / 2nd / 3rd+
Title		
Connections of	Locations	Current companies
Add connection of	Add a location	Add a company

Figure 3.12

Paul Myers, the BBC researcher and creator of Research Clinic, has a vast archive of guides and tips for social media searching and verification of social media. Doug Haddix, long-time journalist and executive director of Investigative Reporters and Editors, also has concise tip sheets. Henk Van Ess, journalist and professor in Europe, shares his tips and guides online, too.

BOX 3.3 Useful Tools for Searching Social Media

Some useful search tools for social media include:

- StalkScan that is a another good search tool for Facebook at https://stalkscan.com/
- AllMyTweets at www.allmytweets.net that gathers all the tweets by a user.
- The LinkedIn search tool can also run searches based on name, company, schools, groups, and location.
- The Social searcher site, at www.social-searcher.com/, collates postings on different social media my topics.
- The TrendsMap at www.trendsmap.com/ shows what topics are trending in Twitter around the world.

The list could be quite lengthy, and there are journalists to follow who keep up with the ever changing tools, some of which disappear because their access to social media is cut off or because a better tool comes along. This book does not cover the more advanced tools that require coding skills, but the Knight Lab at Northwestern University at https://knightlab.northwestern.edu/ is good place to go to get the latest tips on social media tools; the lab itself produces tools for social media analysis and data analysis.

But again it is how you use the tools that matters, and some of the simplest uses can take your reporting to another level.

In one recent example, a former physics graduate student at the University of Illinois in Urbana-Champaign was arrested and charged with kidnapping a young Chinese female scholar. Within 24 hours, using the small amount of information supplied in an FBI affidavit filed in federal court, journalists and interested members of the public had found and posted stories. Among the findings:

- From Christensen's Facebook posting, they gleaned he was from Stevens Point, Wisconsin, what his interests were, that he liked the book "American Psycho," was interested in gaming and, of course, his list of friends and comments about him.
- From his wife's Facebook posting, you could see she had changed her photo the first day he was interrogated by authorities, which replaced the one of both of them at his graduation at the University of Wisconsin in Madison, Wisconsin.
- From the site, Reddit, other sleuths had shared various notes from looking at his website. Since he was a teaching assistant, students also commented on Reddit about contact with him.
- From the dating site, Tinder, he had posted he had an open marriage and described himself.

There are more in-depth stories and investigations that use open source text, video, and audit and worth monitoring and taking their tutorials. A leader in the field is Bellingcat at www.bellingcat.com/ shown in Figure 3.13, where the researchers piece together different parts of unstructured data to investigate such topics as who downed the Malaysian airliner over the Ukraine or who is behind chemical attacks in Syria.

Figure 3.13

Bellingcat also provides instruction and tutorials on how to do these kinds of stories, as shown in Figure 3.14.

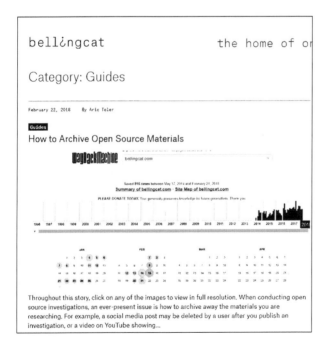

Figure 3.14

Another impressive social media story that came before the stories on Russian **bots** (algorithmic programs that pretend to be real people) was from South Korean journalists a few years ago. In their investigation they found their country's intelligence officers trying to influence elections through social media.

The Korea Center for Investigative Journalism was suspicions about the spy agency's involvement in the presidential election of 2012, which disclosed some 600 Twitter accounts suspected to be related to the spy agency. After studying Social Network Analysis of 280,000 Twitter postings, it revealed that at least ten groups systematically operated on Twitter. The work disclosed the involvement of South Korea's highest-level intelligence agency, which is banned from political activity. The journalists did an excellent slideshare presentation that explained their work at www.slideshare.net/newstapa/south-korean-spy-agencys-illegal-campaigning-on-sns, as shown in Figure 3.15.

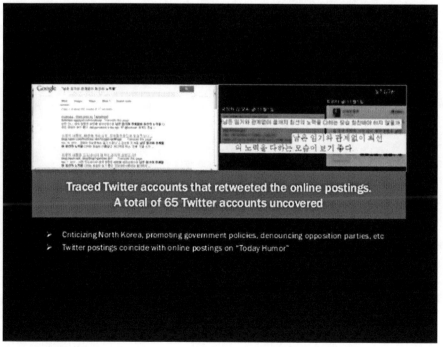

Figure 3.15

Crowd-Sourcing

One other technique to mention is crowd-sourcing. Journalists can put out a general online call for help in getting information on an event or deciphering data, but over the past few years they have been developing a more "form-al" approach, whether it is asking citizens to put information in a Google Form or developing an application as a leader in the field, like ProPublica.org. ProPublica has been able to engage thousands of persons in stories whether they are war veterans, financially stressed homeowners, or many other groups that can help give story tips or personal stories. In one of their more recent efforts, ProPublica developed an application to monitor Facebook ads and whether they are political or not, as shown in Figure 3.16.

Figure 3.16

Authenticity and Accuracy

Throughout this book, we stress being as accurate as possible and being skeptical. In the area of social media, it is of upmost importance to determine who and what is authentic. We have mentioned some of the fact-checking tips and sites, and these will be updated constantly. Keep checking back with those sites so you are keeping current with the latest fakery.

Chapter Summary

- Unstructured data is non-tabular information such as text, video, or audio.
- There are websites and tools to help convert unstructured data in structured data so it can be analyzed more accurately.
- Social media is unstructured data that is valuable for newsgathering and there are digital tools to help search social media better and to analyze.
- Crowd-sourcing has proven an effective way to encourage communities of people to provide personal stories, news tips and help with data analysis.
- Visualization of unstructured data is a necessity because of the large amount of information and data.
- The authenticity of those on social media must be confirmed, as must the information they convey.

Applying CAR

It is well worth getting into more detail about Korean Center's stellar work in finding the country's own spies interfering with politics. Here is a summary.

They received a tip about an online smear campaign by the National Intelligence Service to influence the 2012 elections. With social network analysis software they identified about 600 Twitter accounts and a network of ten groups as held by spies. The center googled 100 postings on a specific site run by the spies and found similar content to that in Twitter. They then traced Twitter accounts that retweeted postings and uncovered another 65 Twitter accounts involved. They also retrieved postings made by deleted Twitter accounts from a weblog and collected 280,000 postings from 450 Twitter accounts. They also tracked down email accounts associated with the Twitter accounts. The center's work led to indictments and reform.

Suggested Exercises

1. Pick a public figure or public official and make up a list of social media sites to check about that official.
2. Use the advanced searches in the social media.
3. Search the social media and keep an organized list of findings and of the public figure or public official's post. See what other resources the social media may lead you to: property records, criminal records, voting records and so on.
4. Test out software that helps locate and collate social media.
5. Come up with three story ideas that could use crowd-sourcing.

Spreadsheets, Part 1
Basic Math for Journalists

4

> Members of the Virginia General Assembly received more than $117,700 in gifts from businesses, special interest groups, and lobbyists, according to computer-assisted research by Virginia Commonwealth University's (VCU's) Legislative Reporting class. The gifts included hunting trips to Georgia, Texas, and even Canada: two senators hunted caribou in the Arctic Circle, courtesy of the Virginia Sheriffs' Association. The most generous benefactor was Philip Morris, which treated lawmakers to almost $26,000 in meals, entertainment, golf equipment, and other freebies. In January, legislators filed reports listing the gifts they received. After creating a database from the reports, VCU students identified the biggest givers and recipients of gifts—and for the first time put the database online so the public can search it.
>
> —Jeff South, *Virginia Commonwealth University*

This story by a college reporting class of Jeff South, a former reporter and current professor, outdistanced the work by professional journalists and received wide attention in the state of Virginia. It also showed how putting information into a spreadsheet for analysis can lead to powerful stories. South's class collected information on the gifts, entered the 1,000 or so records in a spreadsheet, and did simple calculations to find who was giving gifts to legislators. The resulting stories shed new light on the legislators and those who court them.

Journalists use spreadsheets daily, whether it is to pick out patterns of waste and abuse in government or to provide context with figures of information that show the years of data and trends. Using spreadsheets is a particularly attractive approach for journalists beginning to do computer-assisted reporting because it's easy to get data into a spreadsheet format. As noted previously noted, many government agencies around the world—especially census offices—routinely place data files in spreadsheet format so they can be quickly downloaded and analyzed.

It is equally easy to enter data in a spreadsheet from documents when no electronic data exists, as the VCU students showed. (More on building a spreadsheet in Chapter 9.) *The Times-Picayune* in New Orleans, for example, entered information on riverboat pilots, taken from their job applications and resumes, to reveal the nepotism, lack of education, and criminal backgrounds among the pilots. In another instance, *USA Today* built a spreadsheet from information revealed in lawsuits to show the abuse and near-enslavement of immigrants.

Becoming Friendly with Numbers

Journalists constantly report on numbers, although you'll often hear them say they hated math in school—and that they still hate it. Well, many people hate flying on airplanes, but they do it because their jobs require them to do so. Not many of these people become pilots, but they know the plane will take them where they need to go. The same idea applies to modern journalists and spreadsheets. A modern journalist doesn't have to be a mathematician to deal with numbers, but he or she should be willing to use a spreadsheet when needed to get the job done. By not using a spreadsheet, reporters will strain for hours with a calculator trying to figure out whether a government official has hired and given his cronies the largest raises of the year compared to the other employees.

Eric Lipton, a Pulitzer Prize-winning reporter who works for *The New York Times*, discovered the efficiency of spreadsheets while working at *The Hartford Courant*. Lipton, a young reporter at the time, was examining a generous early retirement plan for city employees. He was trying to calculate the **percentage** of each person's pension as compared to his or her salary at the time of retirement. Experts told him the figure should be approximately 67 percent, but in the city's early retirement plan some retirees' pensions came close to the full amount of their former salary.

Lipton was tediously tapping a calculator for each comparison when he remembered that he had seen a spreadsheet demonstration in which repetitive calculations were done much more rapidly. With a little help, he imported the information into a spreadsheet and learned how to do one calculation. Then he copied that calculation for more than 100 other entries. Those calculations served as the starting point for a front-page story.

What Lipton discovered is that a spreadsheet prevents unnecessary repetition and otherwise saves an enormous amount of time and improves accuracy in calculations. A spreadsheet also allows you to quickly figure out such things as who received the most money, who acquired the highest percentage raise, who made the most drug arrests, or which city's housing prices increased the most. Let's take a look at how a spreadsheet can be used for examining pay raises.

You know this year's average raise for an agency's employees is 3 percent. At the same time, you have a list of the political appointments and their wages last year and this year. (All names in this example are fictional.) Figure 4.1 shows a partial list of the official's cronies on the city payroll.

You can see each piece of information is in a box known as a "cell."

As you can see in Figure 4.1, we also have *columns* labeled with letters and *rows* labeled with numbers. This is the key concept of a spreadsheet, and it's one that you have used in other parts of life.

	A	B	C
1	Name	Last year	This year
2	Dee Dale	$ 45,000	$ 52,000
3	Ed Powell	$ 25,000	$ 30,000
4	Jane Deed	$ 14,000	$ 19,000
5	Joe Smith	$ 30,000	$ 39,000
6	Julia Jones	$ 50,000	$ 58,000
7	Mark Forest	$ 15,000	$ 21,000
8	Mary Hill	$ 22,000	$ 29,000
9	Tom Brown	$ 40,000	$ 47,000

Figure 4.1

Learning Addresses

In hard copy road atlases, there is an index. Let's say the index refers you to page 7 and identifies the town's location as D4. The map is laid out in a grid with letters across the top and numbers down the sides. You look down column D and then look across row 4. If you play chess, you use the same kind of grid to keep track of the moves of pieces.

Spreadsheets treat your information as though it's part of a map or grid. So in Figure 4.1 above, the spreadsheet sees the salary not only as $25,000, but also as "B2." So, back to the raises.

Look at the row of Dee Dale. Dale's salary increased from $45,000 to $52,000. The difference isn't too hard to see. It's $7,000. The changes in others' salaries wouldn't be hard to calculate, although if the government official had 100 cronies it would start to get "taxing" (so to speak).

An old-fashioned journalist would analyze raises by taking a calculator and subtracting the information in column B from that in column C. It doesn't take too long to do the calculations for a list of 10 or 20 names, but frequently a journalist is handed a list of hundreds or thousands of names. In Lipton's study of pensions and salaries, he had more than 100 names and was not looking happily ahead to hours of work.

This is where a spreadsheet comes in handy. In a spreadsheet, you would not subtract $45,000 from $52,000. You would subtract B2 from C2. But where would you put it? Well, there's a blank space next to C2, called D2. So, here's the way to do it in a spreadsheet:

As Figure 4.2 shows, move the cursor to box D2 and click on your mouse. Then type: "=C2-B2." Always type the equal sign first so that the spreadsheet knows a formula is coming. (Lower case or upper case does not matter.)

	A	B	C	D
1	Name	Last year	This year	
2	Dee Dale	$ 45,000	$ 52,000	=c2-b2
3	Ed Powell	$ 25,000	$ 30,000	
4	Jane Deed	$ 14,000	$ 19,000	
5	Joe Smith	$ 30,000	$ 39,000	
6	Julia Jones	$ 50,000	$ 58,000	
7	Mark Forest	$ 15,000	$ 21,000	
8	Mary Hill	$ 22,000	$ 29,000	
9	Tom Brown	$ 40,000	$ 47,000	

Figure 4.2

Hit the "Enter" key, and there's the result in Figure 4.3. $7,000.

What you just did is set up a formula—not a complicated one—but a formula nonetheless that does the simple arithmetic for you.

	A	B	C	D
1	Name	Last year	This year	
2	Dee Dale	$ 45,000	$ 52,000	$ 7,000
3	Ed Powell	$ 25,000	$ 30,000	
4	Jane Deed	$ 14,000	$ 19,000	
5	Joe Smith	$ 30,000	$ 39,000	
6	Julia Jones	$ 50,000	$ 58,000	
7	Mark Forest	$ 15,000	$ 21,000	
8	Mary Hill	$ 22,000	$ 29,000	
9	Tom Brown	$ 40,000	$ 47,000	

Figure 4.3

Now you're ready to use the spreadsheet to save time. You want to repeat the formula for every raise. Repeat the formula by copying not $7,000 but "=C3-B3." One way to do this is move the cursor back to D3 and highlight the formula by placing the cursor there and clicking on the cell. Highlight D3 and then move the cursor to the lower right-hand corner of D3 until you see a narrow cross as in Figure 4.4.

	A	B	C	D
1	Name	Last year	This year	
2	Dee Dale	$ 45,000	$ 52,000	$ 7,000
3	Ed Powell	$ 25,000	$ 30,000	
4	Jane Deed	$ 14,000	$ 19,000	
5	Joe Smith	$ 30,000	$ 39,000	
6	Julia Jones	$ 50,000	$ 58,000	
7	Mark Forest	$ 15,000	$ 21,000	
8	Mary Hill	$ 22,000	$ 29,000	
9	Tom Brown	$ 40,000	$ 47,000	

Figure 4.4

Next, define the area you want to copy by clicking the narrow cross on D2, holding down the button on your mouse, and dragging the shading to the last row.

Now let go of the clicker on your mouse, and there are all your numbers. (See Figure 4.5.)

=C2-B2

⊿	A	B	C	D	E
1	Name	Last year	This year		
2	Dee Dale	$ 45,000	$ 52,000	$ 7,000	
3	Ed Powell	$ 25,000	$ 30,000	$ 5,000	
4	Jane Deed	$ 14,000	$ 19,000	$ 5,000	
5	Joe Smith	$ 30,000	$ 39,000	$ 9,000	
6	Julia Jones	$ 50,000	$ 58,000	$ 8,000	
7	Mark Forest	$ 15,000	$ 21,000	$ 6,000	
8	Mary Hill	$ 22,000	$ 29,000	$ 7,000	
9	Tom Brown	$ 40,000	$ 47,000	$ 7,000	
10					

Figure 4.5

What you are doing is telling the spreadsheet to do the same thing it did in D2 for the rest of the rows. Notice the formula =C2-B2 is listed above the worksheet in the line above the numbers so that you know what formula was copied.

As we said, the spreadsheet isn't going to copy $7,000 to every box in the D column. It's going to copy the formula of subtracting the B column from the C column in each row. So it will subtract B4 from C4, B5 from C5, and so on.

Always take a close look at the column after you have copied the formula. (We will label new columns later in this chapter.) If you did copy your formula incorrectly, you will increase your error by the number of rows you copied it to.

Another way to copy your formula—if there are no blank rows—is to double click once you see the narrow cross. When you double click the narrow cross, the formula will be copied and the numbers will be copied and appear until there is a blank row. Then you will have to drag the narrow across the blank row to keep copying.

Calculating Percentages

Let's continue our analysis of the increases. When you look at the salary increases, the largest increase is not necessarily the most important. After all, $5,000 added to $60,000 doesn't have the same impact as $5,000 added to $30,000. Often, you want to know who received the highest percentage increase. This brings you to a bugaboo of many journalists: the **percentage difference**.

Calculating a percentage difference is straightforward if you break it down into its components. If one of the official's cronies is making $45,000 and gets a raise to $52,000, the difference is $7,000. That means you divide 7,000 (the increase) by 45,000 (the original salary): 7,000/$45,000. That gives you 0.155, which is the same as 15.5 percent.

If you were saying it instead of calculating it: "Subtract the first column from the second column and divide the result by the first." In this case, it's $52,000 minus 45,000; then $7,000 divided by $45,000,000. Another way to remember it is what journalists call "NOO," which is the (New–Old)/Old. How would this look in a spreadsheet? Go to your spreadsheet and find the difference: $7,000. That's in cell D3. Where's the old salary? In cell B2. So your formula is D2/B2, as Figure 4.6 shows.

	A	B	C	D	E
1	Name	Last year	This year	Raise	
2	Dee Dale	$ 45,000	$ 52,000	$ 7,000	=D2/B2
3	Ed Powell	$ 25,000	$ 30,000	$ 5,000	
4	Jane Deed	$ 14,000	$ 19,000	$ 5,000	
5	Joe Smith	$ 30,000	$ 39,000	$ 9,000	
6	Julia Jones	$ 50,000	$ 58,000	$ 8,000	
7	Mark Forest	$ 15,000	$ 21,000	$ 6,000	
8	Mary Hill	$ 22,000	$ 29,000	$ 7,000	
9	Tom Brown	$ 40,000	$ 47,000	$ 7,000	

Figure 4.6

Once again, tip-off the spreadsheet that a formula is coming with the equal sign in box E2, type "D2/B2," hit "Enter," and the result appears as Figure 4.7 shows.

=D2/B2

	A	B	C	D	E
1	Name	Last year	This year	Raise	
2	Dee Dale	$ 45,000	$ 52,000	$ 7,000	0.1555556
3	Ed Powell	$ 25,000	$ 30,000	$ 5,000	
4	Jane Deed	$ 14,000	$ 19,000	$ 5,000	
5	Joe Smith	$ 30,000	$ 39,000	$ 9,000	
6	Julia Jones	$ 50,000	$ 58,000	$ 8,000	
7	Mark Forest	$ 15,000	$ 21,000	$ 6,000	
8	Mary Hill	$ 22,000	$ 29,000	$ 7,000	
9	Tom Brown	$ 40,000	$ 47,000	$ 7,000	

Figure 4.7

Again, to save time, copy the formula using the narrow cross. Your result in Figure 4.8 will be:

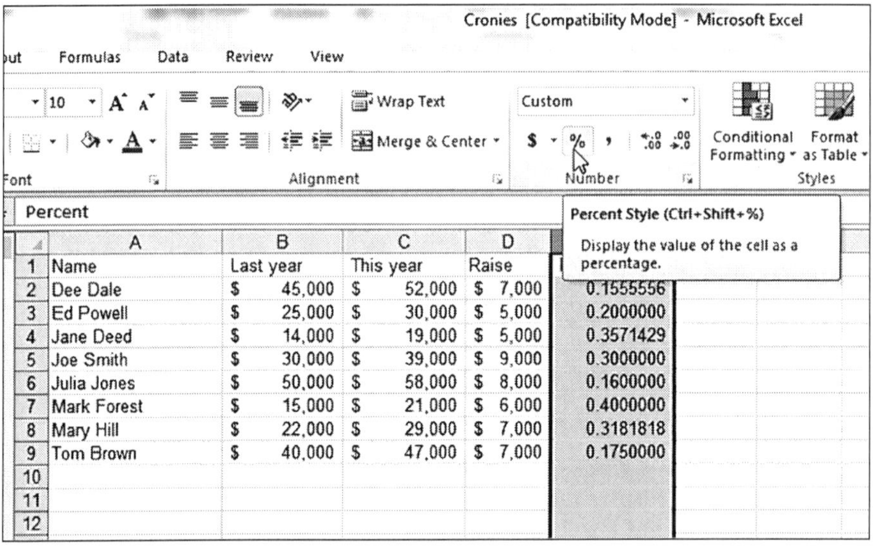

	A	B	C	D	E
1	Name	Last year	This year	Raise	
2	Dee Dale	$ 45,000	$ 52,000	$ 7,000	0.1555556
3	Ed Powell	$ 25,000	$ 30,000	$ 5,000	0.2000000
4	Jane Deed	$ 14,000	$ 19,000	$ 5,000	0.3571429
5	Joe Smith	$ 30,000	$ 39,000	$ 9,000	0.3000000
6	Julia Jones	$ 50,000	$ 58,000	$ 8,000	0.1600000
7	Mark Forest	$ 15,000	$ 21,000	$ 6,000	0.4000000
8	Mary Hill	$ 22,000	$ 29,000	$ 7,000	0.3181818
9	Tom Brown	$ 40,000	$ 47,000	$ 7,000	0.1750000
10					
11					
12					

Figure 4.8

But there are too many numbers to the right of the decimal, and it looks confusing. You would never publish percentages in this form, so you use a handy icon from the spreadsheet. You highlight the column by clicking on the letter E above the top row, moving the cursor onto the percent (%) sign, and clicking on it. (At this point, let's put column labels on the change column and percent column.)

The outcome in Figure 4.9 is much easier to read when you change the numbers into percentages:

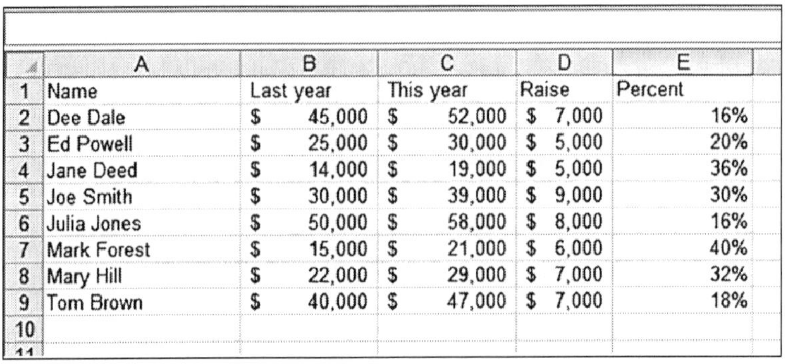

	A	B	C	D	E
1	Name	Last year	This year	Raise	Percent
2	Dee Dale	$ 45,000	$ 52,000	$ 7,000	16%
3	Ed Powell	$ 25,000	$ 30,000	$ 5,000	20%
4	Jane Deed	$ 14,000	$ 19,000	$ 5,000	36%
5	Joe Smith	$ 30,000	$ 39,000	$ 9,000	30%
6	Julia Jones	$ 50,000	$ 58,000	$ 8,000	16%
7	Mark Forest	$ 15,000	$ 21,000	$ 6,000	40%
8	Mary Hill	$ 22,000	$ 29,000	$ 7,000	32%
9	Tom Brown	$ 40,000	$ 47,000	$ 7,000	18%
10					

Figure 4.9

Going from Horizontal to Vertical

By comparing rows, you have been doing calculations horizontally in the two-dimensional world of a spreadsheet. But you also can do vertical calculations. For the story on the official's cronies, you might want to know how much their salaries are costing taxpayers. For this, you want to total numbers in the columns. Move the cursor to the box in Figure 4.10 in which you want the total to appear. You type the equal sign, the word "SUM," in B11 and then the range of cells you want to total. In this case, the numbers start at B2 and end at B9. So you type "=SUM (B2:B9)" as Figure 4.10 shows, putting a colon between the beginning location and the ending location.

=SUM(B2:B9)					
	A	B	C	D	E
1	Name	Last year	This year	Raise	Percent
2	Dee Dale	$ 45,000	$ 52,000	$ 7,000	16%
3	Ed Powell	$ 25,000	$ 30,000	$ 5,000	20%
4	Jane Deed	$ 14,000	$ 19,000	$ 5,000	36%
5	Joe Smith	$ 30,000	$ 39,000	$ 9,000	30%
6	Julia Jones	$ 50,000	$ 58,000	$ 8,000	16%
7	Mark Forest	$ 15,000	$ 21,000	$ 6,000	40%
8	Mary Hill	$ 22,000	$ 29,000	$ 7,000	32%
9	Tom Brown	$ 40,000	$ 47,000	$ 7,000	18%
10					
11	Total	=SUM(B2:B9)			
12					

Figure 4.10

When you hit "Enter," the total appears as in Figure 4.11.

	A	B	C	D	E	F
1	Name	Last year	This year	Raise	Percent	
2	Dee Dale	$ 45,000	$ 52,000	$ 7,000	16%	
3	Ed Powell	$ 25,000	$ 30,000	$ 5,000	20%	
4	Jane Deed	$ 14,000	$ 19,000	$ 5,000	36%	
5	Joe Smith	$ 30,000	$ 39,000	$ 9,000	30%	
6	Julia Jones	$ 50,000	$ 58,000	$ 8,000	16%	
7	Mark Forest	$ 15,000	$ 21,000	$ 6,000	40%	
8	Mary Hill	$ 22,000	$ 29,000	$ 7,000	32%	
9	Tom Brown	$ 40,000	$ 47,000	$ 7,000	18%	
10						
11	Total	$ 241,000				
12						

Figure 4.11

Rather than repeating the formula for each column, do what you did when calculating differences in rows: using the narrow cross, copy the formula horizontally, as shown in Figure 4.12. Remember not to include the percentage column because you are not adding percentages.

=SUM(B2:B9)				
A	B	C	D	E
1 Name	Last year	This year	Raise	Percent
2 Dee Dale	$ 45,000	$ 52,000	$ 7,000	16%
3 Ed Powell	$ 25,000	$ 30,000	$ 5,000	20%
4 Jane Deed	$ 14,000	$ 19,000	$ 5,000	36%
5 Joe Smith	$ 30,000	$ 39,000	$ 9,000	30%
6 Julia Jones	$ 50,000	$ 58,000	$ 8,000	16%
7 Mark Forest	$ 15,000	$ 21,000	$ 6,000	40%
8 Mary Hill	$ 22,000	$ 29,000	$ 7,000	32%
9 Tom Brown	$ 40,000	$ 47,000	$ 7,000	18%
10				
11 Total	$ 241,000			
12				

Figure 4.12

Let go of the mouse button, and the result appears as Figure 4.13 shows.

=SUM(B2:B9)				
A	B	C	D	E
1 Name	Last year	This year	Raise	Percent
2 Dee Dale	$ 45,000	$ 52,000	$ 7,000	16%
3 Ed Powell	$ 25,000	$ 30,000	$ 5,000	20%
4 Jane Deed	$ 14,000	$ 19,000	$ 5,000	36%
5 Joe Smith	$ 30,000	$ 39,000	$ 9,000	30%
6 Julia Jones	$ 50,000	$ 58,000	$ 8,000	16%
7 Mark Forest	$ 15,000	$ 21,000	$ 6,000	40%
8 Mary Hill	$ 22,000	$ 29,000	$ 7,000	32%
9 Tom Brown	$ 40,000	$ 47,000	$ 7,000	18%
10				
11 Total	$ 241,000	$ 295,000	$ 54,000	
12				

Figure 4.13

You might also want to determine how the **average** increase for the official's cronies compares to the average increase for all employees. There are two ways of looking at this. To compare the average percentage increase for the official's cronies, giving equal weight to each employee regardless of salary, you would average the percentages in column E and get 26 percent. (We will do an average later in this chapter.)

But if you wanted to calculate the percentage increase in the total amount of money paid to the cronies, you would calculate the difference in the rows. To do that, you would not average the percentages. You would calculate the percentage difference between the totals (C11 and B11) by subtracting B11 from C11 with the answer appearing in D11. Then, you would divide D11 by B11. The result, as Figure 4.14 shows, would be approximately 22 percent, or more than four times that of all employees.

=D11/B11

	A	B	C	D	E
1	Name	Last year	This year	Raise	Percent
2	Dee Dale	$45,000	$52,000	7,000	13%
3	Ed Powell	$25,000	$30,000	5,000	17%
4	Jane Deed	$14,000	$19,000	5,000	26%
5	Joe Smith	$30,000	$39,000	9,000	23%
6	Julia Jones	$50,000	$58,000	8,000	14%
7	Mark Forest	$15,000	$21,000	6,000	29%
8	Mary Hill	$22,000	$29,000	7,000	24%
9	Tom Brown	$40,000	$47,000	7,000	15%
10					
11	Total	$241,000	$295,000	54,000	22%

Figure 4.14

Comparing Parts to the Sum

You might also want to see who got the biggest chunk of money out of the salary increases. If this were a city budget, you might want to see which department received the largest portion of the city budget. In either case, you want to compare the individual raises with the total amount of raises for each person. Thus, you want to compare D2 with D11, D3 with D11, and so on.

However, a spreadsheet is used to moving down a row at each calculation. Without some hint of what you want to do, the spreadsheet will compare D2 with D11 and then D3 with D12, which would be nonsense. The long and short of it is that we need to "anchor" D11.

Fortunately, spreadsheets give us an easy way to accomplish that. As Figure 4.15 shows, we anchor D11 by putting a dollar sign before the letter and a dollar sign before the number: "$D$11." The first dollar sign anchors the column, and the second dollar sign anchors the row. Now the spreadsheet knows to compare all the numbers in a column only with D11.

=D2/$D$11

	A	B	C	D	E	F
1	Name	Last year	This year	Raise	Percent	Percent of Total
2	Dee Dale	$ 45,000	$ 52,000	$ 7,000	16%	=D2/$D$11
3	Ed Powell	$ 25,000	$ 30,000	$ 5,000	20%	
4	Jane Deed	$ 14,000	$ 19,000	$ 5,000	36%	
5	Joe Smith	$ 30,000	$ 39,000	$ 9,000	30%	
6	Julia Jones	$ 50,000	$ 58,000	$ 8,000	16%	
7	Mark Forest	$ 15,000	$ 21,000	$ 6,000	40%	
8	Mary Hill	$ 22,000	$ 29,000	$ 7,000	32%	
9	Tom Brown	$ 40,000	$ 47,000	$ 7,000	18%	
10						
11	Total	$ 241,000	$ 295,000	$ 54,000	22%	

Figure 4.15

Tap the "Enter" key, and in Figure 4.16 you obtain a new percentage of the total. (Make sure to format the column as percentages as you did before.)

=D2/$D$11

	A	B	C	D	E	F
1	Name	Last year	This year	Raise	Percent	Percent of Total
2	Dee Dale	$ 45,000	$ 52,000	$ 7,000	16%	13%
3	Ed Powell	$ 25,000	$ 30,000	$ 5,000	20%	
4	Jane Deed	$ 14,000	$ 19,000	$ 5,000	36%	
5	Joe Smith	$ 30,000	$ 39,000	$ 9,000	30%	
6	Julia Jones	$ 50,000	$ 58,000	$ 8,000	16%	
7	Mark Forest	$ 15,000	$ 21,000	$ 6,000	40%	
8	Mary Hill	$ 22,000	$ 29,000	$ 7,000	32%	
9	Tom Brown	$ 40,000	$ 47,000	$ 7,000	18%	
10						
11	Total	$ 241,000	$ 295,000	$ 54,000	22%	
12						

Figure 4.16

Again, copy the formula. Figure 4.17 shows the result.

Joe Smith

	A	B	C	D	E	F	G
1	Name	Last year	This year	Raise	Percent	Percent of Total	
2	Dee Dale	$ 45,000	$ 52,000	$ 7,000	16%	13%	
3	Ed Powell	$ 25,000	$ 30,000	$ 5,000	20%	9%	
4	Jane Deed	$ 14,000	$ 19,000	$ 5,000	36%	9%	
5	Joe Smith	$ 30,000	$ 39,000	$ 9,000	30%	17%	
6	Julia Jones	$ 50,000	$ 58,000	$ 8,000	16%	15%	
7	Mark Forest	$ 15,000	$ 21,000	$ 6,000	40%	11%	
8	Mary Hill	$ 22,000	$ 29,000	$ 7,000	32%	13%	
9	Tom Brown	$ 40,000	$ 47,000	$ 7,000	18%	13%	
10							
11	Total	$ 241,000	$ 295,000	$ 54,000	22%		

Figure 4.17

From this calculation you see that Joe Smith got the biggest chunk—17 percent—of the raises.

Sorting the Results

Journalists generally want to analyze and present information in some specific order. If you were doing this with a large spreadsheet, you would have to go through hundreds of numbers to search for the highest percentage. Instead, a spreadsheet allows you to *sort* the information rapidly.

This brings us to another bugaboo. When you sort the information in a spreadsheet, you want to keep all of the information in each row together. But a spreadsheet can make sorting so easy that a journalist can rush past this important point. Many older versions of spreadsheets allowed you to sort one column of information without moving the rest of the row. That meant your percentages were suddenly scrambled and matched against the wrong information. In newer versions, you can get into the same kind of trouble by putting blank columns between columns of information and ignoring the warnings that pop up.

Before sorting, you must make sure that you outline the entire area to sort. All applicable rows and columns of numbers are highlighted. Here you outline the entire area, as Figure 4.18 shows.

Name					
	A	B	C	D	E	F
1	Name	Last year	This year	Raise	Percent	Percent of Total
2	Dee Dale	$ 45,000	$ 52,000	$ 7,000	16%	13%
3	Ed Powell	$ 25,000	$ 30,000	$ 5,000	20%	9%
4	Jane Deed	$ 14,000	$ 19,000	$ 5,000	36%	9%
5	Joe Smith	$ 30,000	$ 39,000	$ 9,000	30%	17%
6	Julia Jones	$ 50,000	$ 58,000	$ 8,000	16%	15%
7	Mark Forest	$ 15,000	$ 21,000	$ 6,000	40%	11%
8	Mary Hill	$ 22,000	$ 29,000	$ 7,000	32%	13%
9	Tom Brown	$ 40,000	$ 47,000	$ 7,000	18%	13%
10						
11	Total	$ 241,000	$ 295,000	$ 54,000	22%	
12						

Figure 4.18

You then decide to go to the "Sort" command under "Data" in the menu (see Figure 4.19).

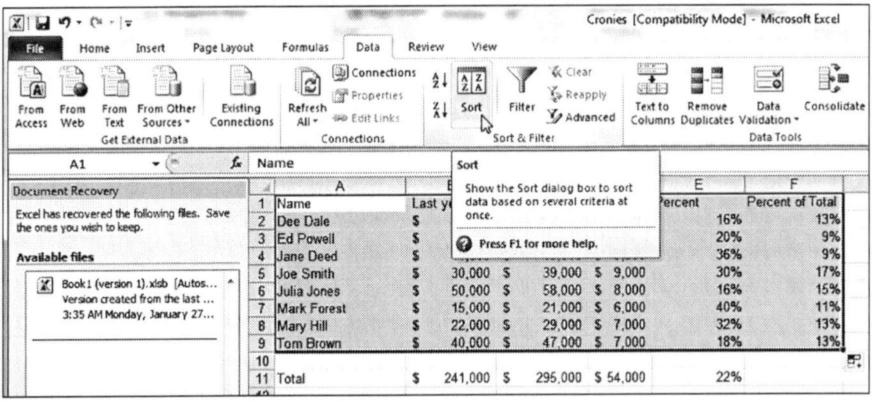

Figure 4.19

Clicking on "Sort" brings up the next screen, which gives the opportunity to choose which column to sort by and in what order. Lowest to highest is called **ascending**, and highest to lowest is called **descending**. You will run into these terms in other programs such as database managers. As Figure 4.20 shows, you choose the "Raise" column and choose "largest to smallest" which means it will be descending order. Note the small box on the top right that says "My data has headers." This means the sort takes into account if you have included the label for each column.

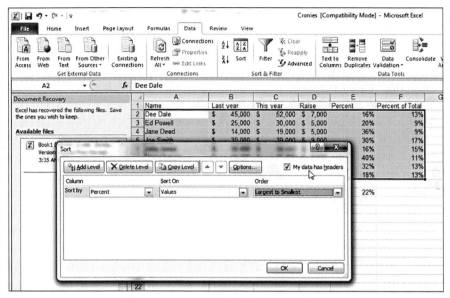

Figure 4.20

Now click "OK." In Figure 4.21 you see that Mark Forest received the highest percentage raise, 40 percent.

	A	B	C	D	E	F	G
	Name	Last year	This year	Raise	Percent	Percent of Total	
1	Name	Last year	This year	Raise	Percent	Percent of Total	
2	Mark Forest	$ 15,000	$ 21,000	$ 6,000	40%	11%	
3	Jane Deed	$ 14,000	$ 19,000	$ 5,000	36%	9%	
4	Mary Hill	$ 22,000	$ 29,000	$ 7,000	32%	13%	
5	Joe Smith	$ 30,000	$ 39,000	$ 9,000	30%	17%	
6	Ed Powell	$ 25,000	$ 30,000	$ 5,000	20%	9%	
7	Tom Brown	$ 40,000	$ 47,000	$ 7,000	18%	13%	
8	Julia Jones	$ 50,000	$ 58,000	$ 8,000	16%	15%	
9	Dee Dale	$ 45,000	$ 52,000	$ 7,000	16%	13%	
10							
11	Total	$ 241,000	$ 295,000	$ 54,000	22%		
12							

Figure 4.21

At this point, your initial work is done, and it's time to start planning your interviews with the official, cronies, and regular employees ... At the same time, you should start planning your graphics and photos to go with the story.

Using Average and Median for Better Accuracy

To deal with numbers, you should know three of the most common ways of summarizing a collection of numbers: **mean, median**, and **mode**. *Mean* is what is commonly called the average. *Median* is defined as the middle value, or the point at which half the numbers fall above and half the numbers fall below. (If there is a tie, it gets a little tricky, but a spreadsheet can work out the calculation for you.) *Mode* is the value that most frequently appears.

Neill Borowski, another data journalism pioneer who practiced and taught data analysis at *The Philadelphia Inquirer*, used a good example of this at a national conference. He said baseball players' salaries outraged fans because fans always heard the average salary was $1.2 million. But the median salary was $500,000, and the mode, or the most frequent salary, was $109,000.

Those numbers indicate that there are a few players making really big money. The median, or middle, value, the salary amount that half the salaries exceed and half the salaries fall below, was $500,000. If you asked all baseball players for a count of hands for each salary, the largest number (the *mode*, not the majority) of hands would go up for $109,000. (Okay, it's still a great deal, but not as much as you thought. And it's being made by people generally making most of their money in 10 years or fewer.)

Journalists want to make sure they represent numbers as fairly and accurately as possible, and these three ways of looking at numbers give them a chance to do so. If a journalist obtains a set of salaries, house prices, or test scores, he or she needs to consider what the fairest representation is. If the numbers are relatively close together, the mean (or average) is a reasonable way to summarize them. But if the numbers are spread out, a journalist doesn't want a few bad apples, or very rich apples, to distort the summary and so a median is better . . .

Let's stay on the subject of sports and take a look at a professional basketball team. (You could select any superstars in any sport for any country in this example.) Figure 4.22 shows what the players make (a fictional amount) in the first quarter of each game.

▲	A	B	C
1	The Team		
2	Player	Salary	
3	Player A	70000	
4	Superstar	60000	
5	Player B	40000	
6	Player C	30000	
7	Player D	50000	
8			

Figure 4.22

First, we will get the average of what they make. You get an average by going to B8 and typing the formula =AVERAGE (B3:B7) as shown in Figure 4.23 and hitting Enter.

=AVERAGE(B2:B7)

	A	B
1	The Team	
2	Player	Salary
3	Player A	70000
4	Superstar	60000
5	Player B	40000
6	Player C	30000
7	Player D	50000
8		=AVERAGE(B2:B7)

Figure 4.23

You will see you will get 50,000. Next, we will get the median of what they make. You obtain a median by going to B9 and typing the formula =MEDIAN (B3:B7) as shown in Figure 4.24.

=MEDIAN(b2:b7)

	A	B
1	The Team	
2	Player	Salary
3	Player A	70000
4	Superstar	60000
5	Player B	40000
6	Player C	30000
7	Player D	50000
8		50000
9		=MEDIAN(b2:b7)
10		

Figure 4.24

You will get 50,000 again and at this point, there is no difference between average and median because for median there are two salaries higher than $50,000 and two salaries lower than $50,000. Now, let's say we look back at our figures and realize we left a zero off the superstar's salary. We replace his salary of $60,000 with $600,000 as in Figure 4.25.

=AVERAGE(B2:B7)

	A	B
1	The Team	
2	Player	Salary
3	Player A	70000
4	Superstar	600000
5	Player B	40000
6	Player C	30000
7	Player D	50000
8	AVERAGE	158000
9	MEDIAN	50000

Figure 4.25

Notice how the formula immediately changes the result in average. The median does not change because there are still two salaries higher and two salaries lower than $50,000. This is an extreme example, but you can see that the median more fairly represents what the players make since only the superstar makes six figures per quarter.

Interpreting Outliers

In this example, the superstar would be considered an **outlier**. In social research parlance, an *outlier* is a number that is out on the edge, or way up on the top of the chart or way down at the bottom of the chart.

These measurements—average and median—help you quickly identify an outlier. You could say that the superstar, the chief executive of the corporation, makes more than ten times as much as the median wage.

But, quite often, if you examine a few databases closely, you begin to regard outliers with healthy suspicion. Outliers often are too good to be true. They frequently turn out to be the product of data-entry errors, which will be examine later. The usual disappointment is that someone erroneously put in an extra zero, for example, and a salary actually is $60,000.

Also, social scientists suggest that you look carefully at the outliers and possibly discard them, especially if you expect to work with averages. That doesn't mean you can't bring the outliers back for a repeat performance later. You might be looking at U.S. Census data and notice that one county has highly unusual numbers. So you first examine the data for all of the counties except for that one in your first analysis. Then, you look at the data for all of the counties together to see how that one county can distort the numbers.

Averages can also hide important information. At the *San Jose Mercury News*, in a classic story, reporters obtained an electronic file from the city that included the times of the alarms and the times of fire trucks' arrival at the scene of fires. The fire department claimed that its average response time was four and a half minutes, half a minute under the maximum time it allowed to get to any fire.

Reporters Betty Barnacle and Chris Schmitt found the fire department wasn't wrong about its average. What the fire department didn't say—but the numbers showed—was that on one-fourth of its calls, the fire department exceeded its 5-minute maximum response time. With his analysis, Schmitt ensured that the story not only related information about an isolated occurrence, but also showed a pattern of problems.

Chapter Summary

- Spreadsheets can help you do calculations faster and more easily.
- Spreadsheets use letters to identify columns and numbers to identify rows.
- For calculations, spreadsheets allow you to use column letters and row numbers to create formulas.
- When you are comparing the parts of a calculation with the sum, don't forget to "anchor" the sum.
- Percentage difference often provides a more fair comparison than the actual change in numbers.
- When you sort, make sure to highlight the entire range of numbers that you want to sort.
- Take into consideration the best number to use—mean or median. And don't forget the impact of any outliers on your calculation.

Applying CAR

When a court reporter at *The Hartford Courant*, Jack Ewing, and I looked at racial disparities in bail for criminal defendants in Connecticut, we examined the average bail for blacks and Hispanics versus whites. However, on the advice of some good social science researchers, we limited the bail to amounts above zero and equal to or below $100,000. (We got rid of zero because that meant the person did not have any bail set. We held to $100,000 or below because there were a few amounts above $100,000 that could distort the results.) We found that black and Hispanic males, on average, received much higher bail—nearly double— than whites for the same kind of felony. Then, we went back and looked at the outliers. It turned out that an unusual number of high bail amounts were being given to blacks in one courthouse. In fact, blacks were getting higher bail amounts—as much as $1,000,000—for drug charges than some whites were getting for drug charges or murder.

Later, a judge in New Haven acknowledged that he was giving out high bail to those accused of drug offenses because he didn't think the accused spent enough time in jail once they were convicted. Thus, his solution was to lock up the presumed innocent. Unfortunately, the judge was contributing to his own frustration because when he kept people in jail awaiting trial, it created prison overcrowding —which led to the early release of those found guilty and serving time. He was unaware, however, that he also was creating racial disparities.

Once again, we learned how numbers and math can not only provide context, but also can tip us to a good stories. Using a spreadsheet to do a few calculations, it's possible to find patterns, make better comparisons, and discover the unusual.

Suggested Exercises

1. Get a list of names and salaries from your local government or region in electronic form.
2. Also get a part of a government budget in electronic form. Make sure you get 2 years' worth.
3. Put the data sets into a Microsoft Excel worksheet.
4. Sort in descending order using the salaries from the salary dataset. Sort in descending order using the amount of each budget row from the budget dataset.
5. Calculate the difference in the budget years. Calculate the percentage difference.
6. Calculate the total, average, and median for the salaries.
7. Find out which department receives the largest percentage of the budget.

Spreadsheets, Part 2

More Math that Matters

5

We decided to obtain a list of the delinquent taxpayers, analyze it and publish it in a format that people could understand . . . the top ten real estate debtors combined owed more than $6.4 million but the city is unlikely to collect any of that soon.

— *The Waterbury Republican American* in Connecticut

Simply summing the two columns showed what the campaign spent and took in . . . Overall we found at least $10,000 in unaccounted funds and several violations of state election law.

— *The Courier-Post* in New Jersey

Simply put, a ratio study compares assessed values with actual prices properties sell for . . . We got a county overseer to admit that his assessors were murmuring privately about so many mistakes . . . it's unbelievable.

— *Pittsburgh Tribune-Review* in Pennsylvania

In recent years, journalists have gone beyond their basic math and also used data management to reveal stories. They calculate a rate and a ratio; filter and reconfigure data to make it more meaningful; and visualize using charts and graphs. Most often, they do this using spreadsheet software.

Journalists also are using statistical software, such as SPSS, SAS, or R (also called GNU S) and applying the social research methods espoused by Philip Meyer, a pioneer in database analysis and author of *Precision Journalism*.

In the previous chapter, we looked at the basic math a journalist needs to know and how spreadsheets make doing that math faster and easier. This chapter will expand on the basic math and statistic skills for achieving better journalism.

Rates

Sarah Cohen, a Pulitzer Prize-winning reporter and former government statistics expert, says, "Rates are used to level the playing field."

Rates allow you to make comparisons that are more fair and accurate—just as calculations of the median or percentage difference do. Just comparing raw numbers can wrongly and unfairly distort the differences on such topics as illnesses, traffic accidents, and crimes. Ten traffic accidents in an intersection in which only 100 cars pass through a day has a far different impact than ten traffic accidents at an intersection in which 10,000 cars pass a day. Consequently, journalists now calculate rates on many topics such as transportation accidents, taxes, deaths, loans, arrests, and disease. Let's take a look at crime data as an example.

If you were to look at crime statistics on murder a few years ago in U.S. cities larger than 250,000 in population, it would probably not surprise you that Chicago leads with 500 murders and New York is close behind with 419 (see Figure 5.1). After all, Chicago and New York are both are cities with large populations.

	C2	f_x 500	
	A	B	C
1	City	Population	Murders
2	Chicago	2,708,382	500
3	New York	8,289,415	419
4	Detroit	707,096	386
5	Philadelphia	1,538,957	331
6	Los Angeles	3,855,122	299
7	Baltimore	625,474	218
8	Houston	2,177,273	217
9	New Orleans	362,874	193
10	Dallas	1,241,549	154

Figure 5.1

But would that really tell you how dangerous Chicago would be compared to other cities? Would it give you an idea of the relative chances of being murdered in Chicago as compared to another city? Not really. One way to get a better idea is to use a per capita figure or a rate. Now that you know formulas, you know how easy it is to do a calculation in a spreadsheet.

In Figure 5.2, you divide the number of murders in each city (C2 for Chicago) by each city's population (B2). This would give you a per capita (per person) figure; however, all of those decimals would prevent it from being meaningful to a reader or viewer.

	D2			f_x	=C2/B2	
	A		B		C	D
1	City		Population		Murders	
2	Chicago		2,708,382		500	0.00018
3	New York		8,289,415		419	
4	Detroit		707,096		386	
5	Philadelphia		1,538,957		331	
6	Los Angeles		3,855,122		299	
7	Baltimore		625,474		218	
8	Houston		2,177,273		217	
9	New Orleans		362,874		193	
10	Dallas		1,241,549		154	

Figure 5.2

To make it more understandable, you need to move the decimal point to the right. You can do this by multiplying the per capita figure by 100,000 to get the rate per 100,000 persons. The multiplier is often a judgment on what makes sense, such as the population size and the number of occurrences in relation to the population (see Figure 5.3).

	SUM		X ✓ f_x	=C2/B2*100000		
	A		B	C	D	E
1	City		Population	Murders		
2	Chicago		2,708,382	500	=C2/B2*100000	
3	New York		8,289,415	419		
4	Detroit		707,096	386		
5	Philadelphia		1,538,957	331		
6	Los Angeles		3,855,122	299		
7	Baltimore		625,474	218		
8	Houston		2,177,273	217		
9	New Orleans		362,874	193		
10	Dallas		1,241,549	154		

Figure 5.3

Then, by multiplying by 100,000 you get 18.46121 as shown in Figure 5.4.

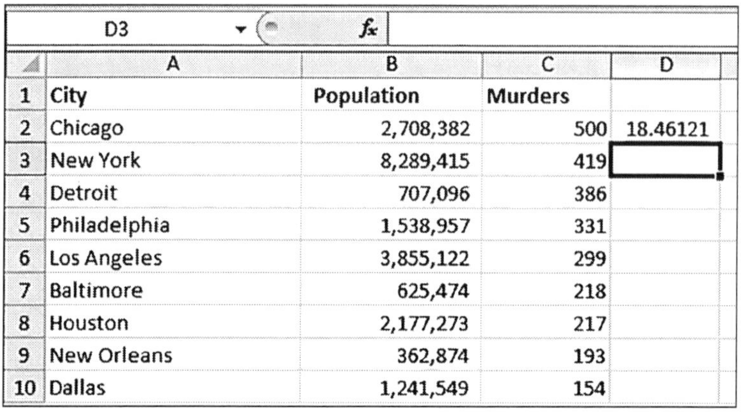

D3		f_x	
	A	B	C	D
1	City	Population	Murders	
2	Chicago	2,708,382	500	18.46121
3	New York	8,289,415	419	
4	Detroit	707,096	386	
5	Philadelphia	1,538,957	331	
6	Los Angeles	3,855,122	299	
7	Baltimore	625,474	218	
8	Houston	2,177,273	217	
9	New Orleans	362,874	193	
10	Dallas	1,241,549	154	

Figure 5.4

After you get the formula, copy it down the column with the narrow cross to obtain figures for each city (see Figure 5.5). (A helpful hint: also, click on the "," in the tool bar to reduce the decimals to only two places. This should automatically appear in your tool bar as shown in Figure 5.5.)

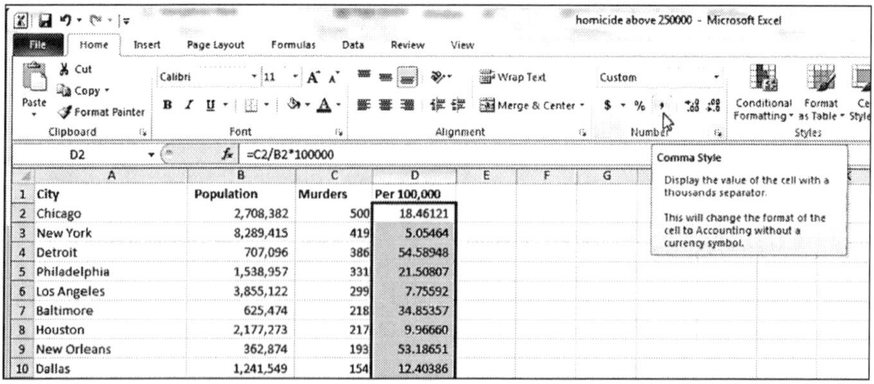

homicide above 250000 - Microsoft Excel

D2 f_x =C2/B2*100000

	A	B	C	D	E	F	G
1	City	Population	Murders	Per 100,000			
2	Chicago	2,708,382	500	18.46121			
3	New York	8,289,415	419	5.05464			
4	Detroit	707,096	386	54.58948			
5	Philadelphia	1,538,957	331	21.50807			
6	Los Angeles	3,855,122	299	7.75592			
7	Baltimore	625,474	218	34.85357			
8	Houston	2,177,273	217	9.96660			
9	New Orleans	362,874	193	53.18651			
10	Dallas	1,241,549	154	12.40386			

Comma Style

Display the value of the cell with a thousands separator.

This will change the format of the cell to Accounting without a currency symbol.

Figure 5.5

Now, sort the information in descending order by the column labelled "Per 100,000" as shown in Figure 5.6. (Don't forget to select the entire data range so that columns are not accidentally sorted out of order.)

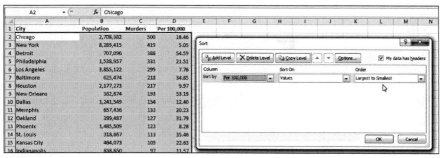

Figure 5.6

You will find, as shown in Figures 5.7a and b, that Detroit has the most murders per 100,000 people at 54.59, Chicago, at 18.46, falls in thirteenth place, and New York's rate is 5.05, which puts it in 54th place. This gives you some idea of the likelihood of a murder occurring in Detroit as compared to these other cities. Of course, you would need to do further analysis to see what parts of the city the murders occurred.

	D2	▼	f_x =C2/B2*100000
	A	**B**	**C**	**D**
1	City	Population	Murders	Per 100,000
2	Detroit	707,096	386	54.59
3	New Orleans	362,874	193	53.19
4	St. Louis	318,667	113	35.46
5	Baltimore	625,474	218	34.85
6	Newark	278,906	96	34.42
7	Oakland	399,487	127	31.79
8	Stockton	299,105	71	23.74
9	Kansas City	464,073	105	22.63
10	Philadelphia	1,538,957	331	21.51
11	Cleveland	393,781	84	21.33
12	Memphis	657,436	133	20.23
13	Atlanta	437,041	83	18.99
14	Chicago	2,708,382	500	18.46
15	Buffalo	262,434	48	18.29

Figure 5.7a

50	Wichita	386,409	23	5.95
51	Fort Worth	770,101	44	5.71
52	Las Vegas Metropolitan Po	1,479,393	76	5.14
53	Corpus Christi	312,565	16	5.12
54	Riverside	313,532	16	5.10
55	New York	8,289,415	419	5.05

Figure 5.7b

Ranking

Once you have the worksheet organized this way, you might want
to rank the cities; that is, list the cities from high to low as based on
your work. To do this, you first create a new column by highlighting
Column A and then clicking on Insert to create a new column as in
Figure 5.8.

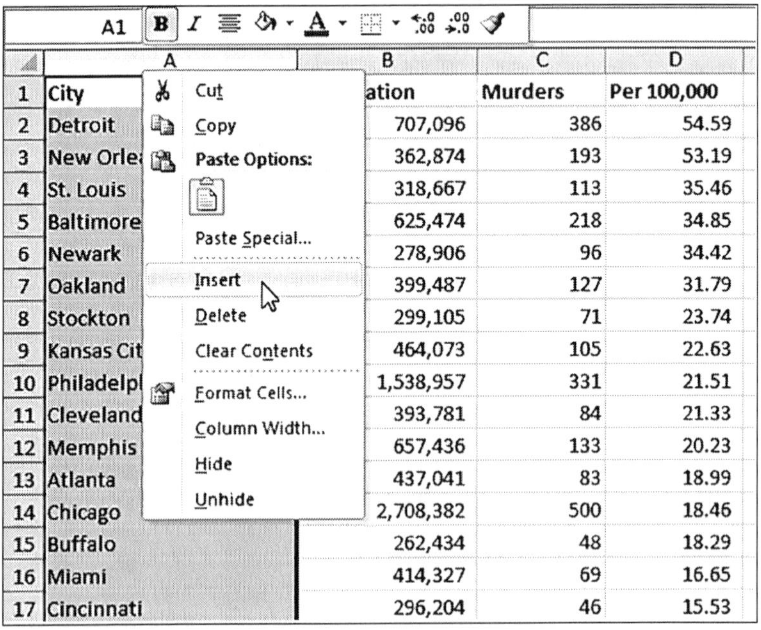

Figure 5.8

By clicking on Insert, you get a new column to the left of the cities as in Figure 5.9 and you can type in a column title, "Rank."

	A1	▾	× ✓ ƒx	Rank		

	A	B	C	D	E
1	Rank	City	Population	Murders	Per 100,000
2		Detroit	707,096	386	54.59
3	�	New Orleans	362,874	193	53.19
4		St. Louis	318,667	113	35.46
5		Baltimore	625,474	218	34.85
6		Newark	278,906	96	34.42
7		Oakland	399,487	127	31.79
8		Stockton	299,105	71	23.74
9		Kansas City	464,073	105	22.63
10		Philadelphia	1,538,957	331	21.51
11		Cleveland	393,781	84	21.33

Figure 5.9

Now type 1 in A2 and 2 in A3 as shown in Figure 5.10.

	A3	▾	× ✓ ƒx	2		

	A	B	C	D	E
1	Rank	City	Population	Murders	Per 100,000
2		1 Detroit	707,096	386	54.59
3	2	New Orleans	362,874	193	53.19
4		St. Louis	318,667	113	35.46
5		Baltimore	625,474	218	34.85
6		Newark	278,906	96	34.42
7		Oakland	399,487	127	31.79
8		Stockton	299,105	71	23.74
9		Kansas City	464,073	105	22.63
10		Philadelphia	1,538,957	331	21.51
11		Cleveland	393,781	84	21.33

Figure 5.10

Highlight both A2 and A3 and place the cursor in the lower-right-hand corner of A3 as shown in Figure 5.11 so that you see the narrow cross.

A2		▼	fx	1	
	A	B	C	D	E
1	Rank	City	Population	Murders	Per 100,000
2	1	Detroit	707,096	386	54.59
3	2	New Orleans	362,874	193	53.19
4		St. Louis	318,667	113	35.46
5		Baltimore	625,474	218	34.85
6		Newark	278,906	96	34.42
7		Oakland	399,487	127	31.79
8		Stockton	299,105	71	23.74
9		Kansas City	464,073	105	22.63
10		Philadelphia	1,538,957	331	21.51
11		Cleveland	393,781	84	21.33

Figure 5.11

Double click on the narrow cross, and you will have a ranking for each city as shown in Figure 5.12. This allows you to provide readers or viewers with an idea of how their city compares to other cities in terms of murders.

	A	B	C	D	E
1	Rank	City	Population	Murders	Per 100,000
2	1	Detroit	707,096	386	54.59
3	2	New Orleans	362,874	193	53.19
4	3	St. Louis	318,667	113	35.46
5	4	Baltimore	625,474	218	34.85
6	5	Newark	278,906	96	34.42
7	6	Oakland	399,487	127	31.79
8	7	Stockton	299,105	71	23.74
9	8	Kansas City	464,073	105	22.63
10	9	Philadelphia	1,538,957	331	21.51
11	10	Cleveland	393,781	84	21.33

Figure 5.12

Filtering

After creating rates and ranks for all the cities, you might want to compare only the largest cities. Without creating a new worksheet, you can use the Filter function of the spreadsheet. That is, you can filter in or filter out the data you want depending on the criteria, just as you would in a Google Advanced Search.

Go to the tool bar and click on Data, as you did when you wanted to Sort. Except this time, choose Filter and click on it. (You must have at least one cell in the worksheet highlighted when you click on Filter.)

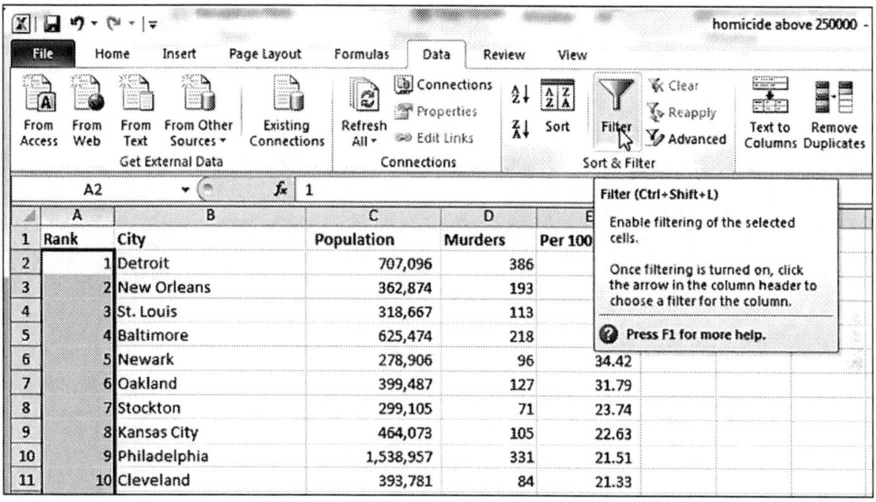

Figure 5.13

By clicking on Filter, you create small scroll arrows for each column. Click on that arrow and then click on Number Filters and choose how you will "filter" the worksheet; for instance, "as greater than or equal to" as shown in Figure 5.14.

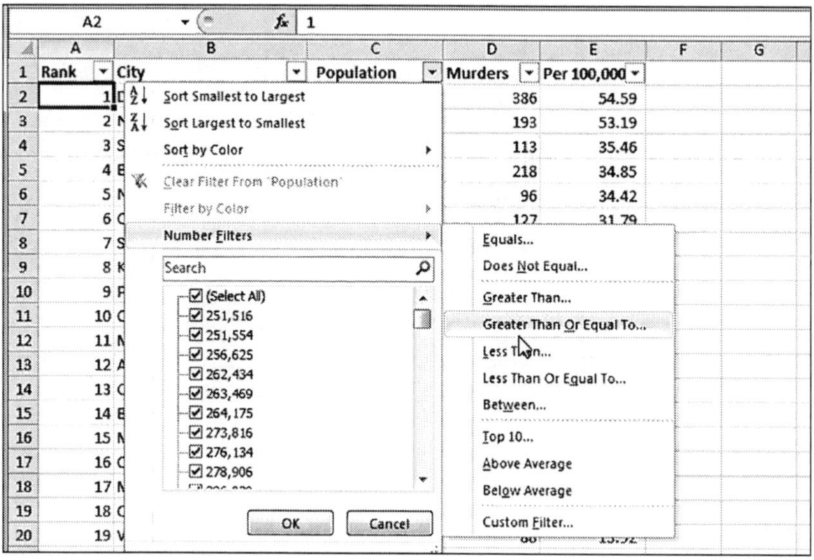

Figure 5.14

Click on the arrow next to "greater than or equal to" as in Figure 5.15, and you will get a box to place a number in.

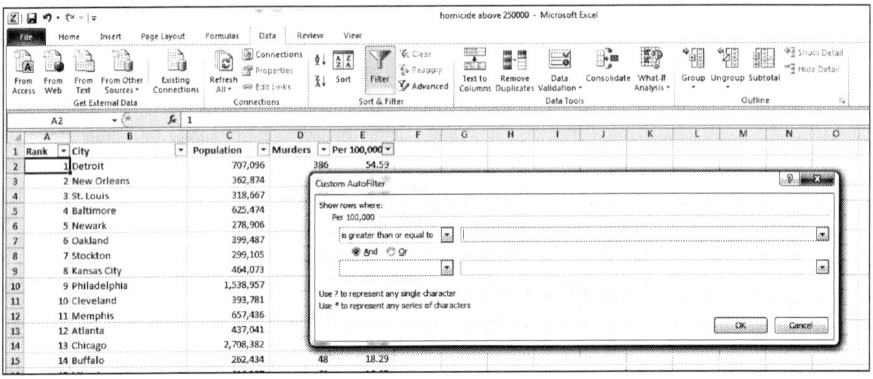

Figure 5.15

Now, type 1,000,000 as in Figure 5.16. (Note that this box uses Boolean logic—and, or, not—mentioned in Chapter 2, which allows you to employ more specific criteria.) This kind of filtering of information based on a criterion will be discussed again in Chapter 6 on database managers. In database software, filtering is known as choosing the criteria or using a **where statement**.

Figure 5.16

Click OK. You now will have a much smaller set of data comparing cities with populations with 1,000,000 persons or more. Note that Chicago in now in second place and New York is in ninth place as shown in Figure 5.17.

	A2	▾	f_x	1	

◢	A	B	C	D	E
1	Rank ▾	City ▾	Population	▾ Murders ▾	Per 100,000 ▾
10	9	Philadelphia	1,538,957	331	21.51
14	13	Chicago	2,708,382	500	18.46
24	23	Dallas	1,241,549	154	12.40
31	30	Houston	2,177,273	217	9.97
39	38	Phoenix	1,485,509	123	8.28
41	40	Los Angeles	3,855,122	299	7.76
47	46	San Antonio	1,380,123	89	6.45
52	51	Las Vegas Metropolitan Pc	1,479,393	76	5.14
55	54	New York	8,289,415	419	5.05
68	67	San Diego	1,338,477	47	3.51

Figure 5.17

Ratios

A *ratio* is another simple but powerful calculation to make comparisons that can be more understandable. For example, a ratio can provide one number that can show the difference in the chances of being in an accident, getting a disease, or receiving a grant.

Journalists looking into home mortgage loans have used ratio to illuminate the disparity in loans made by banks to whites and to minorities. If 30 percent of black applicants for loans are denied loans and 10 percent of whites are denied loans, a ratio comes in handy.

Let's calculate only this ratio in a spreadsheet as shown in Figure 5.18. Type Black in A2 and White in B2 and Ratio in C2. Type 30 in A3 and 10 in B3. In C3, type =A3/B3 and hit Enter and you have your ratio of 3 to 1.

	C3	▾	f_x	=A3/B3	

◢	A	B	C	D	E
1	Ratios				
2	Black	White	Ratio		
3	30	10	3		
4					

Figure 5.18

Now, you can convey the disparity more simply by saying that three times as many blacks as whites are denied loans.

Or in another simplified example, you could look at bail disparity using a brief sample data set. In Figure 5.19, you have nine individuals who have had bail set while they await trial for a burglary charge. These are first time offenses and their personal and financial backgrounds are quite similar.

	A	B	C	D
1	Bail	Black	White	Hispanic
2	Accused	40000	15000	42000
3	Accused	45000	20000	45000
4	Accused	50000	25000	42000
5				
6	Average	45000	20000	43000

Figure 5.19

If you calculate the average for each ethnicity, you will see the amount of bail set for black and Hispanics is more than double that for whites as shown in Figure 5.20.

=D6/C6

	A	B	C	D	E	F
1	Bail	Black	White	Hispanic	Ratio - Black to White	Ratio = Hispanic to White
2	Accused	40000	15000	42000		
3	Accused	45000	20000	45000		
4	Accused	50000	25000	42000		
5						
6	Average	45000	20000	43000	2.25	2.15
7						

Figure 5.20

Pivot Tables

We have used "sum" to total columns of numbers, but often we also need summarize data. By that we mean that we need to do a subtotal of numbers by each group within a data set. For example, you might need to summarize the total cost of employee salaries in each agency of a department.

In another example, you might be adding up all the salaries of 25 players on each of 20 teams. That means that you would take a total of 500 rows of information and reduce them to 20 rows of subtotals.

Often, in looking at campaign financial records, journalists want to sum up how much each contributor gave to candidates, or how much each candidate collected in contributions. To do this in a spreadsheet, use a **Pivot Table** because it allows you to get all those subtotals in one overall calculation. Let's say we have a list of political contributors as shown in Figure 5.21.

	A	B	C	D	E	F	G	H	I
	A2	▾	fx	GRUBB					
1	LAST	REST	CITY	STATE	ZIP	OCCUPATION	CONT_DATE	AMOUNT	CAND_ID
2	GRUBB	KITTY	KNOXVILLE	TN	37920	ATTORNEY	10/5/2011	1000	H0TN02017
3	DUNCAN	RICHARD	KNOXVILLE	TN	37919	ATTORNEY	11/23/2011	200	H0TN02017
4	NORTON	FRANKLIN	KNOXVILLE	TN	37901	ATTORNEY	11/2/2011	200	H0TN02017
5	WHELCHEL	BARBARA	KNOXVILLE	TN	37922	HOUSEWIFE	9/28/2011	1000	H0TN02017
6	WHELCHEL	WARD	KNOXVILLE	TN	37939	ATTORNEY	9/28/2011	1000	H0TN02017
7	SHIPLEY	ROBERT	KNOXVILLE	TN	37917	MACHINIST	11/2/2011	200	H0TN02017
8	HARDING	SAMUEL Y	KNOXVILLE	TN	37919	CLOTHING DIST	9/15/2011	200	H0TN02017
9	FURROW	SAM	KNOXVILLE	TN	37901	FURROW AUCTION COMPANY	7/22/2011	500	H2GA08038
10	GENTRY	MACK A	KNOXVILLE	TN	37901	GENTRY AND TIPTON	8/23/2011	250	H2GA08038
11	CONLEY	WILLIAM M	KNOXVILLE	TN	37915	REGAL GROUP	2/25/2011	1000	H2TN03052
12	WARDLEY	J A	KNOXVILLE	TN	37922	SELF/NOVA INC	3/29/2011	1000	H2TN06014
13	MILLIGAN	JAMES	KNOXVILLE	TN	37902	ATTORNEY	8/5/2011	1000	H2TN07038
14	CONLEY	DEANE W	KNOXVILLE	TN	37915	HOMEMAKER	10/25/2011	1000	H2TN07038
15	BRASFIELD	TRAVIS	KNOXVILLE	TN	37912	RETIRED	6/7/2011	1000	H2TN07038
16	GRAVES	JOHN	KNOXVILLE	TN	37922	ATTORNEY	9/9/2011	500	H2TN07038
17	CONLEY	WILLIAM	KNOXVILLE	TN	37915	REGAL CORPORATION	9/22/2011	1000	H2TN07038
18	LOCKETT	CHARLES	KNOXVILLE	TN	37901	ATTORNEY	9/12/2011	250	H2TN07038
19	HOLLAND	TERRY	KNOXVILLE	TN	37923	ATTORNEY	9/9/2011	500	H2TN07038
20	CONLEY	WILLIAM	KNOXVILLE	TN	37915	REGAL CORPORATION	9/22/2011	1000	H2TN07038
21	WORTHINGTON	ROBERT F	KNOXVILLE	TN	37901	BAKER, WORTHINGTON, CROSSLEY, STAN	11/17/2011	500	H2TX00015
22	VIAR	C WILSON JR AND HELEN P	KNOXVILLE	TN	37923	ATTORNEY	11/12/2011	2000	H4MS01052
23	JUBRAN	RAJA	KNOXVILLE	TN	37921	DENARK-SMITH INC	11/16/2011	500	H4TN03033
24	ALDER	MIKE	KNOXVILLE	TN	37918		12/15/2011	250	H4TN03033
25	BRABSON	ALAN	KNOXVILLE	TN	37919	APPALACHIAN APPRAISALS	11/4/2011	500	H4TN03058

Figure 5.21

We see that we have contributors' last names, first and middle names, ZIP code, where they are from, their occupations, a contribution date, the amount they gave, and the ID of the candidate they gave to. (We will make good use of the Candidate ID in the database manager chapters 6 and 7.)

We might want to find out how each contributor gave to a candidate, how much each occupation contributed, or how much came from each ZIP code. A Pivot Table will allow us to perform these calculations. To use a Pivot Table, first go to Insert on the menu bar and click on "Pivot Tables" as in Figure 5.22.

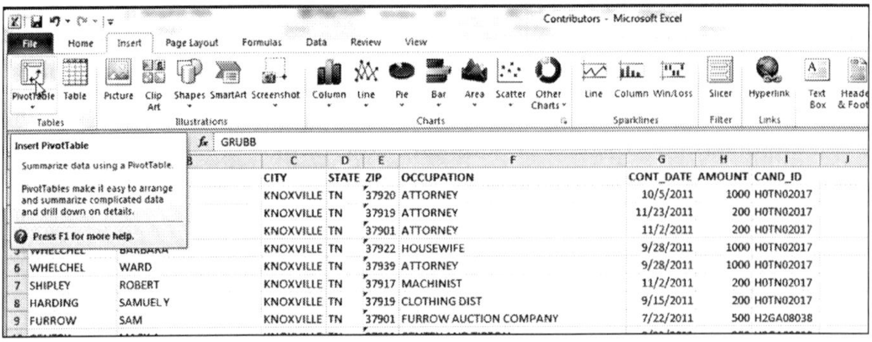

Figure 5.22

You want to make sure you have a cell highlighted in the worksheet when you click on Pivot Table. That means Excel will automatically choose the range of all your data. It should be $A$1 through $G$542 as shown in Figure 5.23.

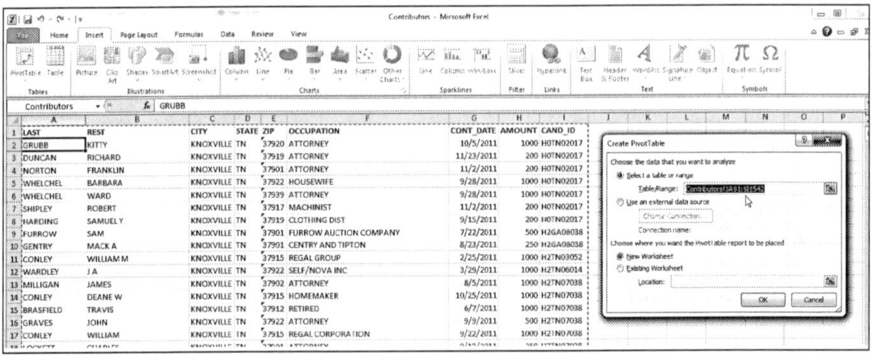

Figure 5.23

Click on OK and the next screen is the template for the Pivot Table as seen in Figure 5.24. You may want to take a minute or two to get oriented. On the right side, you can see that you have the names of your columns in the upper window and the lower window has places to do calculations. On the left side you have the area where you can "build" your pivot table. (For purposes of illustration, the right side and left side have been moved closer together. Something you can do yourself.)

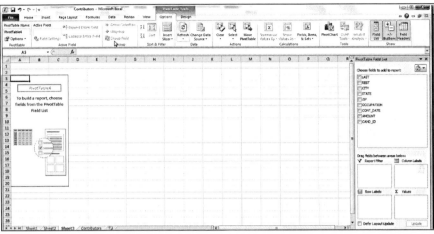

Figure 5.24

For your first summary of data, click on LAST in the right-hand box. You will notice that "LAST" now appears in the right-hand box under Labels. On the left side is a column containing every unique last name (see Figure 5.25).

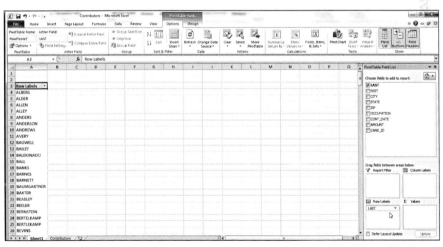

Figure 5.25

If you were to scroll down you would see that 542 rows have crunched into 285 rows of names because there are several rows with the same last name. To see the total given by each of the persons with the same last name you should click on the box next to AMOUNT in the upper-right right-hand box. You will see that Sum of AMOUNT appears in the lower-right-hand box under

Values. On the left side, you have a second column called Sum of
AMOUNT with a total given by each person with the same last
name (see Figure 5.26).

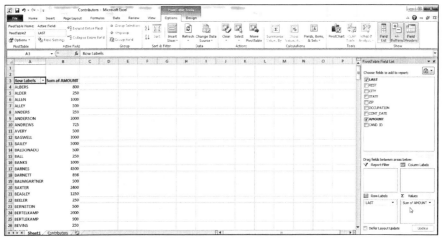

Figure 5.26

To sort the Sum of AMOUNT, highlight the first record in the
second column, which reads 800, click on Data in the Menu Bar,
and then click on "Z to A," which means the data will be sorted
from the highest to lowest amount (see Figure 5.27).

Row Labels	Sum of AMOUNT
ALBERS	800
ALDER	250
ALLEN	1000
ALLEY	500
ANDERS	250
ANDERSON	2000
ANDREWS	725
AVERY	500
BAGWELL	3000
BAILEY	5000

Figure 5.27

After you click on the "Z to A" button, you will now have your data sorted, and you will see that the name "Haslam" and the highest total, "29,500," rise to the top. You can also do this by going to the Data tab and doing the more detailed sorting as in Figure 5.28.

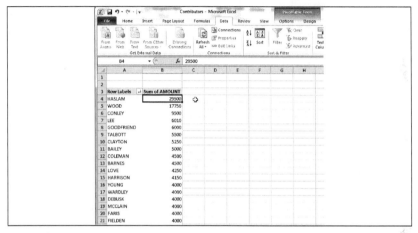

Figure 5.28

If you want to count the number of contributions rather than the amount, you can click on the Sum of AMOUNT in the lower-right-hand side and click on Value Field Settings as in Figure 5.29.

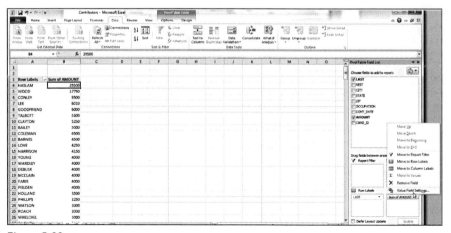

Figure 5.29

Click on Value Field Settings, and you will get a choice of calculations. You should pick "Count" as shown in Figure 5.30.

Figure 5.30

When you click on "Count," the data in Sum of AMOUNT column will change to the number of donations (see Figure 5.31).

Figure 5.31

If you want both a column of sum of amounts and a column of count of donations, you can drag AMOUNT to the lower box so you have two AMOUNTS. The second one will default to Sum of AMOUNT and add the third column to your Pivot Table as Figure 5.32.

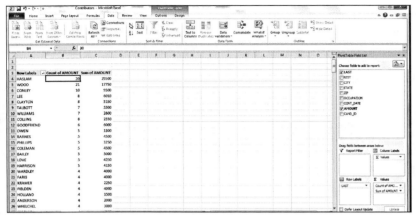

Figure 5.32

There are many other kinds of analyses you can do with a Pivot Table, but this gives you an idea of its power and potential.

Pivot Tables also are good preparation for working with database manager software. With each tool, you are "grouping" similar kinds of information together and totaling the amount. In a database manager, which handles many more records in an easier fashion, this is known as the **"group by"** function. In a database manager, you would "group by" NAME in the previous example and "Sum" the amounts.

Graphs and Charts

There is one last activity to do that can make all the difference in spreadsheets: visually displaying the results of your analysis graphically. By using visualizations, you see differences instantly and don't have to slog through columns and rows of calculations. Spreadsheets permit you to easily place information into bar charts or pie charts and many other kinds of charts.

Using the data discussed above, you could chart the data set of cronies to see which employee received the highest percentages, clearly illustrating this information in a bar chart.

First, highlight the Name column. Then, holding down the control key, move the cursor to the Percent (of raises) column and highlight that column. Then click on Insert in the upper tool bar and. You will see that you can pick from different types of bar charts as shown in Figure 5.33.

File	Home	Insert	Page Layout	Formulas	Data	Review	View	ArcG

PivotTable Table   Picture Clip   Shapes SmartArt Screenshot   Column Line   Pie   Bar   A
                              Art

Tables   Illustrations   Charts

2	Name	Last year	This year	Raise	Percentage Change
3	Dee Dale	$ 45,000	$ 52,000	$ 7,000	16%
4	Ed Powell	$ 25,000	$ 30,000	$ 5,000	20%
5	Jane Deed	$ 14,000	$ 19,000	$ 5,000	36%
6	Joe Smith	$ 30,000	$ 39,000	$ 9,000	30%
7	Julia Jones	$ 50,000	$ 58,000	$ 8,000	16%
8	Mark Forest	$ 15,000	$ 21,000	$ 6,000	40%
9	Mary Hill	$ 22,000	$ 29,000	$ 7,000	32%
10	Tom Brown	$ 40,000	$ 47,000	$ 7,000	18%
11					
12	Total	$ 241,000	$ 295,000	$ 54,000	
13					

Figure 5.33

Click on the bar chart of columns and pick the first one at the top. You will instantly get a bar chart showing the differences in the percentage of raises the cronies received (see Figure 5.34). Furthermore, it is a chart that you can enlarge, move around, or copy and paste. (Note that you can save the chart in its own worksheet.)

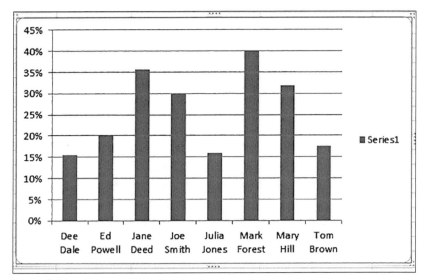

Figure 5.34

You can similarly display increases in crime with a bar chart or easily represent a budget with a pie chart. Sometimes, doing this helps you see the results of your work more clearly. For example, residents of a city may believe they are paying too much for sewer and water services. They claim that commercial businesses use more water and put a burden on the sewer system but don't pay their fair share. You could obtain the budget figures for revenue from the division and put them on a spreadsheet, as shown in Figure 5.35.

Water and sewer division	Last year	This year
Residential water fees	$ 13,235,122.00	$ 18,405,222.00
Residential sewer fees	$ 6,544,344.00	$ 8,324,555.00
Commercial water fees	$ 10,882,021.00	$ 11,504,302.00
Commercial sewer fees	$ 4,343,123.00	$ 5,662,131.00
Investment interest	$ 1,222,494.00	$ 1,445,214.00

Figure 5.35

You can format these figures in a pie chart by choosing that graphic. This will show what kind of percentage and proportion the amounts have, as in Figure 5.36, and make it clear whether the residents may have a legitimate complaint.

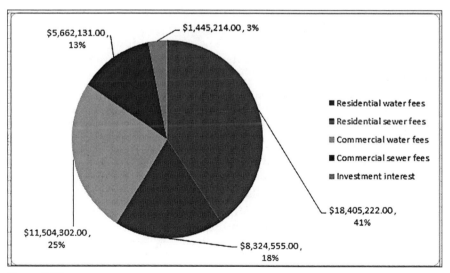

Figure 5.36

As you can see, spreadsheets can provide detailed analysis and comparisons as well as vivid graphics that make it easier to understand the results. After some practice with spreadsheets, you will be ready to move to database managers, where some of the same analyses can be done, but much more quickly and with many more records. Most important, files (known as tables in database managers) can be joined and columns from different files can be used to create a new database.

Chapter Summary

- The use of rates and ratios is a way to fairly compare entities with different populations.
- Spreadsheets allow you to narrow your analysis by filtering the information you want to use.
- Pivot tables give you a way to total information by categories.
- Charts allow you to clearly visualize information and effectively present your findings.

Applying CAR

During the past decade, West Virginia education officials closed one of every five schools in a massive consolidation drive. Parents and opponents said rural children were forced to ride the bus 4 hours a day or longer. State officials said most children rode the bus for only a short time.

We started with asking a simple question: "How long are children's bus rides in West Virginia?" When we looked for electronic records we found that most school districts in 35 rural counties did not keep computerized records. So we obtained the paper records from the counties and built our own database in Excel that included when each run started, when it stopped, and how much time spent in between. Excel was the right tool because we were doing calculations involving the differences in time.

We found the number of children who rode the bus more than 2 hours a day had doubled. Also, we found that two-thirds of the bus routes carrying elementary schoolchildren exceeded the state guidelines that said children should not be on a bus longer than an hour a day.

The state transportation director promised to computerize all records and conduct his own study.

—Scott Fine and Eric Eyre,
The Charleston Gazette

Suggested Exercises

1. Find the crime statistics on the FBI website and download information in a worksheet on crime by year throughout the United States.
2. Open the file in Excel and calculate the crime rates, using the number of crimes and the populations, for violent crimes and for property crimes.
3. Do a ratio of property crimes each year to violent crimes each year.
4. Create a pie chart of property crimes and violent crimes from the most recent year.
5. Download campaign finance information from the Center for Responsive Politics.
6. Use a Pivot Table to illustrate which party received the most funds.

Database Managers, Part 1

Searching and Summarizing

6

> Just how big is the legal gambling industry in Ohio and in the nation, we wondered, and what impact have casinos, multi-state lotteries and other forms of betting in neighboring states had on Ohio? The Ohio Lottery Commission provided an electronic database of sales from stores that sold lottery tickets for the past several years. That made it fairly easy to analyze sales by ZIP codes with Microsoft Access. Using that database and other statistics, The Dispatch was able to estimate that a large chunk of $9.9 billion in revenue from Ohioans' gambling went to neighboring states.
>
> —Barnet D. Wolf, *Columbus Dispatch*

This story involved large databases and many categories of information that a spreadsheet could handle but was simpler to analyze with the database manager Microsoft Access—and could have been done in DB Browser SQLite—because it is easier to select the columns you want to work with and to quickly make subsets of information to analyze.

Many journalists have initially used a database manager to analyze campaign finance records. These records are public and they cross over many topics because campaign finance records are a way of tracking access and influence of contributors on issues such as education, health, business and environment. (Also, in the U.S. the data are kept in relational database of four tables that are joined by ID numbers of candidates and committees. See Chapter 7 for more.)

BOX 6.1 **Purposes of a Database Manager**

The overall value of learning to use a database manager is that it can:

- examine hundreds of thousands of records efficiently;
- allow a reporter to quickly select only certain columns and certain records;
- organize the records into similar groups and sum and count the numbers in those groups;
- compare records in one table with those in one or more other tables. Reporters use a database manager to do what they call the "heavy lifting" of data; that is, searching, summarizing and matching large databases.

You can get these records from public agencies or from non-partisan, nonprofit groups that standardize the data, add additional information, and make them easy to use. In some instances, journalists create their own database.

For decades, journalists conscientiously kept tabs on campaign contributions to politicians. Some kept lists, some kept index cards, and some kept the information in their head. But with the advent of databases, journalists began downloading the data and analyzing it in a spreadsheet or database manager.

In addition to the ease with which a journalist can select certain columns and records from a database, a journalist should learn to use a database manager as soon as possible for one major technical reasons Many databases are kept in several or more tables, as in the case of U.S. Federal Election Commission, which is known as a **relational database**. As mentioned earlier, a relational database has two or more tables (files) that have to be joined by common elements such as ID numbers. So you need to know how to use a database manager in order to analyze that kind of data.

By using databases to monitor campaign donations and expenditures, journalists get a good selection of stories to consider and can readily see how data analysis can lead to a story. Furthermore, many editors support doing stories on this particular topic because most consider it required public service to monitor campaign finance and explain how it influences governmental actions and business.

In addition, a campaign finance database can be used for longer analytical stories while serving as an instant resource for daily stories. After an election ends, a reporter can do a story on how much money the winner received and from whom the winner received it. Then, after the winner takes office and begins to award no-bid contracts, the reporter, using a database manager, can quickly link the recipients of the generous contracts to campaign contributors. A typical headline may read: "Governor's supporters get lucrative contracts."

Another reason campaign contributions are good fodder for learning database managers is because you initially have to concentrate on only a few columns of information. Who gave, how much and to whom (see Figure 6.1).

Contributor	Contribution	Candidate

Figure 6.1

For purposes of this chapter and Chapter 7, we will use a somewhat modified version of real data. It is a classic database used for teaching over the years because it not uses only real data from U.S. federal election database, but it contains many of the shortcomings common to databases such as misspellings and using one column for more than one kind of information.

It is a database on campaign contributions to Congressional candidates in Knoxville, Tennessee in the United States.

To see the data in the database manager DB Browser SQLite, we open the program and then open the database "Politicalcontributions.db." DB Browser is free software that can be downloaded and used on PCs and Macs and other platforms. It has its quirks but it is a common way in which journalists are learning to use database managers. Microsoft Access also is often used by journalists, but there is no version for Macs.

Microsoft Access has a visual way of analyzing the data, called Query by Example, but the main language in database managers is Structured Query Language, known as SQL and often pronounced "sequel," so we will mostly use it in this chapter and the next.

But back to the data as shown in Figure 6.2, where the database "Political Contributions" has been opened.

Figure 6.2

Notice that there are two files known as Tables. This means that a Database itself is like a folder. It can contain one or more tables, often intended to be used together. Click on Candidates and then "Browse Data" as shown in Figure 6.3, and you can see the data of 31 records in that table.

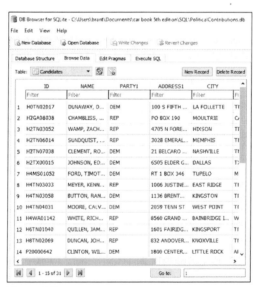

Figure 6.3

It looks much like a spreadsheet but the field names (columns are known as fields in database managers) are embedded. Database managers are meant to be used by more than one person, so the software makes it difficult to change column names or the layout of the data.

Notice that you no longer have letters and numbers to guide you. One difference between spreadsheets and database managers is that information in the former usually comes to you in some sort of order. In the latter, the information initially may be in a random order because the software assumes you will reorder the information constantly. Furthermore, database manager programs aren't set up to copy formulas, which is why spreadsheets have **addresses** of numbers and letters.

After reviewing the field names and data, open the other table by clicking on the scroll button toward the top of the screen as in Figure 6.4.

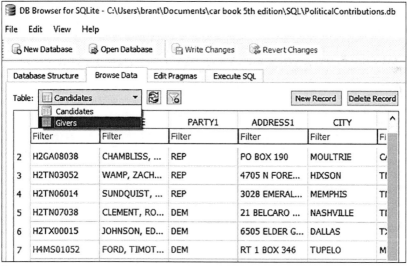

Figure 6.4

After clicking on Givers, you will see in Figure 6.5 the numerous contributors who gave to the 31 candidates in the candidates table. The 541 contributors listed are just a sample from that election, but it is enough to work with and learn "queries" of the data that could be applied to any database. Note that Givers is the same dataset you worked with in the last spreadsheet chapter.

File	Edit	View	Help

New Database   Open Database   Write Changes   Revert Changes

Database Structure	Browse Data	Edit Pragmas	Execute SQL

Table: Givers   New Record   Delete Re

	LAST	REST	CITY	STATE	ZIP
	Filter	Filter	Filter	Filter	Filter
1	GRUBB	KITTY	KNOXVILLE	TN	37920
2	DUNCAN	RICHARD	KNOXVILLE	TN	37919
3	NORTON	FRANKLIN	KNOXVILLE	TN	37901
4	WHELCHEL	BARBARA	KNOXVILLE	TN	37922
5	WHELCHEL	WARD	KNOXVILLE	TN	37939
6	SHIPLEY	ROBERT	KNOXVILLE	TN	37917
7	HARDING	SAMUEL Y	KNOXVILLE	TN	37919
8	FURROW	SAM	KNOXVILLE	TN	37901
9	GENTRY	MACK A	KNOXVILLE	TN	37901
10	CONLEY	WILLIAM M	KNOXVILLE	TN	37915

Figure 6.5

The two tables are meant to be joined by a "key field." In this case, the key field in CAND_ID in the Givers table, or the ID number that is given to the candidate by the Federal Election Commission. In the candidates table, the name of the field that has the candidate ID numbers is called ID. You can see those table structures by clicking on Database Structure and looking at the record layout as in Figure 6.6. Both ID and CAND_ID are marked.

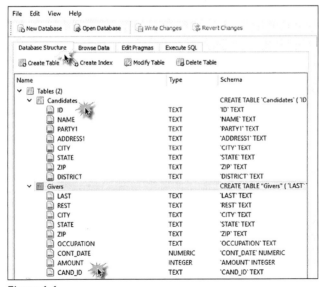

Figure 6.6

You may ask why the data was not all placed in one table. Putting the data in two tables saved time because the candidate information had to be typed only once (31 times) as opposed 541 times (the number required for each contribution record). This is also known as a many-to-one relationship since there are many givers linked to each of the candidates.

It also allows the data about the same topic to be stored efficiently in one table. This linkage will come into play in Chapter 7, but for now we will concentrate on dealing with one table at a time.

The Query

The way you do analysis of a database is to "build" a query.

Unlike a spreadsheet, a database manager is more formal when you want to use it for analysis. Instead of doing your work on the original data, the database manager has you create a "**query**" in a different screen and then has you "run" the query to create a new and temporary table. In DB Browser, you click on the tab "Execute SQL" and you get a blank window in which to write your query as in Figure 6.7.

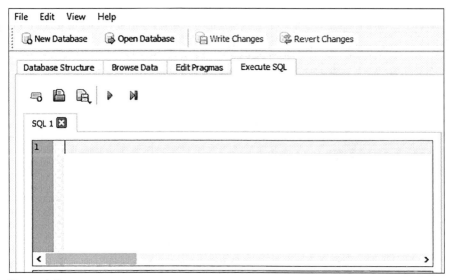

Figure 6.7

BOX 6.2 The Six Commands

There are just six basic commands in SQL.

SELECT—allows you to choose the fields (columns) you want in any order you want

FROM—allows you to choose the table or tables from which you want to use data

WHERE—allows you to select records (rows) you want based on certain criteria and to use Boolean logic

GROUP BY—allows you group data into categories and total each category by summing or counting as you do in a pivot table in a spreadsheet

HAVING—allows you to limit the number of results in a GROUP BY based on a criteria as you would do with WHERE for individual records

ORDER BY—allows you to sort the data from high to low or low to high

Type in the Query Box the basic query that allows you look at all the data in Givers, as shown in Figure 6.8.

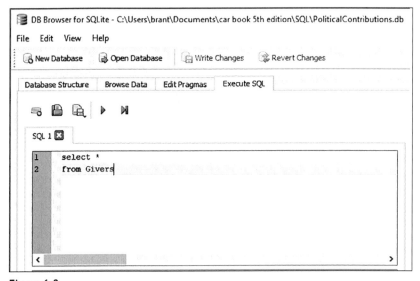

Figure 6.8

Select * chooses all the fields. **From** Givers chooses the table.

Click on the forward (play button) as in Figure 6.9 to run the query.

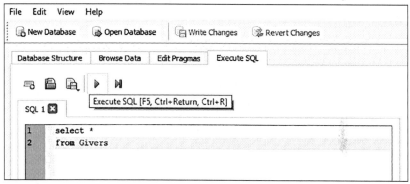

Figure 6.9

After you "run" the query, you will get the results, which shows you every field and record in the Givers table as shown in Figure 6.10.

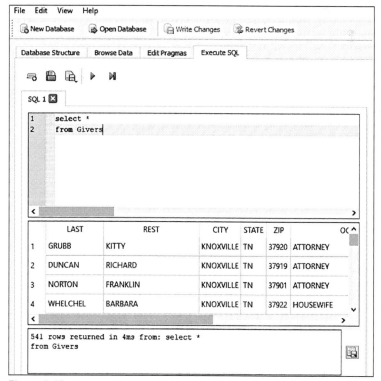

Figure 6.10

Selecting and Searching

A strength of a database manager is speedy *searches*. If you want to find a name, you tell the database manager that you want to look for all the information on that particular name.

First, you select the columns you want to use. The concept of *"select"* allows you to cull through the columns in a database. Often, government databases have 30 or more columns of information. Selection of the fields is important because it clears away distractions. Furthermore, many journalists' analyses eventually involve only four to six fields as they focus by creating subsets of information.

In Figure 6.11, you need to select only three fields—the Rest, Last, Amount—to see who gave how much.

Use the select statement to choose the specific fields and use from again to draw from the Givers table. Then use the play button to get your results as in Figure 6.11.

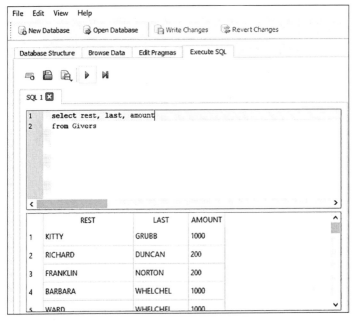

Figure 6.11

We have not lost any of the other information in Table called "givers," but have simply selected three fields temporarily to show in our answer. This "vertical" cut of the information, that is, choosing fields (columns), shows us how easy it is to include some information and exclude other information in the horizontal order we want. If we don't save this result, it will simply disappear when we return to the original information.

Criteria and Filtering

After looking at the fields, you might want to look just at the contributors who gave more than $500. The idea is the same as in Chapter 4, where you used the "Filter" in Excel to limit the information you received.

Return to the query box just add Where "Amount" ">500" as shown in Figure 6.12 and run the query and you get your new results.

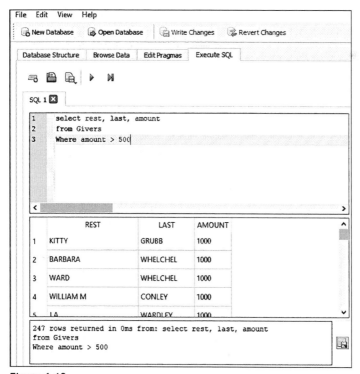

Figure 6.12

Note that the DB Browser also shows you how many records—247—that meet the criteria. (A helpful hint: when you type a number such as 1000, do not put in any commas or the some programs may not read it correctly.)

Sorting

If you want to sort the contributions from highest to lowest, you use the same principle as in the spreadsheet. Return to your query box and type "**Order By**" and then "3 desc". The three refers to the third column—amount—and desc means high to low. Click on the play button and you get your result in Figure 6.13.

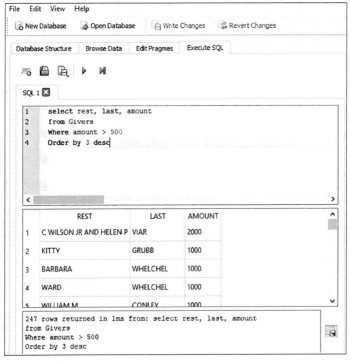

Figure 6.13

Criteria and Wildcards

Spreadsheets allow you to single out one individual record or a batch of records by using filters. In the database manager the filters are in "where" statements—where Last = "Haslam." But database managers also have another powerful filtering function called "like." "Like" lets you choose a name using only a few letters of the name. Because data entry can be an error-prone endeavor, names are often spelled in several different ways in governmental databases. Using "like" is one way to get around the problems.

As shown in Figure 6.14, you can look for all the Haslams by using "like" and something known as a wildcard. You have already seen one wildcard—the asterisk *—used in the select command. (By the way, get rid of >500 in the criteria line to see all contributions by the HASLAMS.)

Like a joker in a deck of cards, this can stand for anything. But the wildcard in DB Browser for the where command is the percentage sign %. so the wildcard after "HASL%" stands for all the numbers or letters that might follow the letters "HASL." (Lower or upper case doesn't matter.)

In Figure 6.14, you type in like "HASL%" in the where line. Then you run the query.

Figure 6.14

By the way, by default DB Browser is case sensitive so if you were looking for "HASLAM" and used lower case or a combination of lower and higher case, you would not get any results if you used an = sign.

But this query picks up every name that begins with the letters "HASL." ensuring that you didn't miss any misspellings in the table and it turns out there was a data entry error and if you scroll down you will see HASLAM was also entered as HASLEM.

Boolean Logic: And, Or, Not

Another strength of database managers is that the search can easily incorporate two or more criteria in a query. To do that, you use the logic we spoke about in Chapter 2—Boolean logic. Some modern librarians call it "a life skill." It also is a routine way of doing online searches.

Boolean logic uses the words *and, or,* and *not.* Those three little words are incredibly powerful.

You might want to search for everyone who is an attorney or housewife who gave more than $500. Boolean logic treats the search in this way: give me everyone who donated who is a housewife *"or"* an attorney *"and"* who gave more than $500.

User-friendly database managers actually are making it easy to do Boolean logic. You would write "where (occupation like "surgeon" or occupation like "attorney") and amount >500." Fields in text always have quotes around them and DB Browser can be a little quirky with the = sign, so it is good to use like instead.

You have to pay attention to your *"ors"* and *"ands"* and be very careful with *"nots."* If you are choosing items in the same field, you don't write: where city = "New York" *and* city = "Los Angeles." How can you be in two places at once? In fact, with that question, you are nowhere at all.

Also as a general rule, if you are choosing items in the same field, put parentheses around them. For example, if you are looking for all the murderers in New York City or Los Angeles, you would write: city = ("New York" or "Los Angeles") and crime = "murderers." If you write: city = "New York" or city = "Los Angeles" and crime = "murderers," you would probably get all the criminals in New York City and all the murderers in Los Angeles.

"Not" is particularly handy when you want to exclude a set of information. If you are analyzing an election in Wisconsin and you wanted to look at only out-of-state contributors, you would use a "not." You would write a query that said: where state = "*not*" "Wisconsin."

Let's return to our table on the contributions and give it a try with query form by looking for every attorney or housewife who gave more than $500. As shown in Figure 6.15, we will delete the current fields in the query box and type occupation = "ATTORNEY" or occupation like "HOUSEWIFE" in parentheses and AMOUNT >500. We put the parentheses around the "or" statement so just those occupations are chosen. Otherwise you would get every attorney and housewife and everyone who gave more than $500. Note that we type the occupations in upper case as they are in the table.

This query translates to wanting to see the name of everyone whose occupation is attorney or surgeon and gave more than $500.

If we run the query, we get the results shown in Figure 6.15.

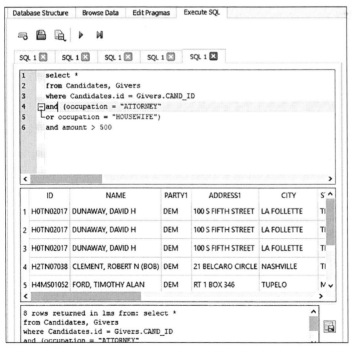

Figure 6.15

Grouping

Once you have selected your fields, set your criteria, and then sorted, you still might want to know which occupation gave the most money. This is where the idea of grouping, or as it's known in database parlance "group by" comes in.

"Group by" is the way to quickly summarize data to look for patterns, trends, outliers, and even errors in the data. Like a pivot table, this is one of the sharpest tools that a journalist can use and accomplishes the same goal as pivot tables in spreadsheets, but once learned can be more efficient.

First, we decide what category (field) we want to "group by" and what field we want to add up. In this example, we want to total the "amount" for each "OCCUPATION." We must always have the fields we are using in the Select line. The trick is that we have to plan ahead. We know we want to sum by each occupation so we will create a new column in the select statement by writing sum (amount).

As in Figure 6.16, where the query and result are shown, we can also make sure to have the results sorted without having to re-do

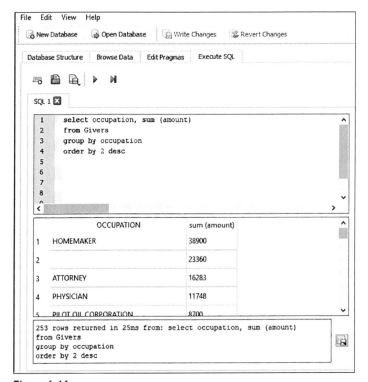

Figure 6.16

the query and thus we can put in ORDER BY 2 desc, which means descending, to sort the result from the high to low amounts.

Your query can actually give you some questions to ask. Why is homemaker the biggest contributing occupation? Why is the second most not identified and is anything being done to make those contributors disclose their occupation? And who runs Pilot Oil Corporation?

You also can count the total number of contributions by using "group by." It's a bit trickier because the best way to count items in a table is to type count (*) in the field name. By using this method, you will count not only the fields filled in, but also the blank fields. If there is a blank field in occupation, many database managers will not count it because the database manager does not count blanks unless you use count (*), as in Figure 6.17.

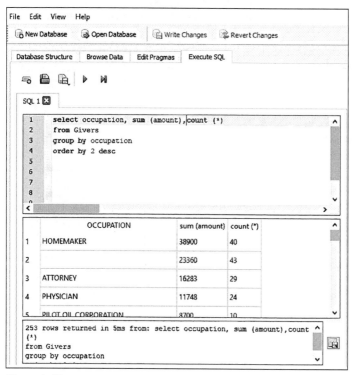

Figure 6.17

Once you feel comfortable with these different queries, you will use a query that has been the basis for many computer-assisted reporting stories. You obtain information, you divide the information into groups, you count or sum parts of the information by groups, and you sort your results from highest to lowest. (In the midst of the query, you may filter in or filter out information with "where" statements.)

You could look at a prison population, divide into ethnicities, and then count the numbers to find the percentage of ethnicities. You could then compare it to the percentage of minorities in the community.

You could look at blighted properties in your city, divide the information into neighborhoods, and then count the number of blighted properties in each neighborhood. You could take thousands of records of federal contracts in your state, divide the information by communities in which work is being done, sum the amounts of the contracts, and then get an idea of the federal contracts' economic importance to those communities. You could look at records of toxic chemical emissions by manufacturers into the environment, divide the information by communities, sum the emissions by communities, and then find out which community has the most toxic releases.

Much of the information you collect can be examined in this way. With this basic information, you start your traditional reporting—interviews and site visits—at an advanced level. With the analysis of the relevant databases, you already have seen trends and patterns, seen the unusual—the "outliers," and are already thinking of follow-up questions to the data. It is as though you are a tipster or an inside source called you on the phone and told you what you should look at. Except that the tipster is not a person, it's database.

In the next chapter, we will look at working with relational databases. The upcoming skills will show you how to compare tables to come up with unique stories and will give you even more control in analyzing data.

Chapter Summary

- Database managers handle large numbers of records and allow you to quickly organize the data the way you want.
- Database managers can do speedy searches for particular information.
- Database managers allow you to easily filter information through one criterion and many criteria.
- Database managers can swiftly create summary data by "grouping" categories of information and allowing you to total the numbers or items in those groups.

Applying CAR

Compared to other dates, Georgia may still struggle to shore up weak public school academic records, but schools and taxpayers spare little expense to field competitive football teams.

We built a comprehensive database of the nearly 2,400 high school football coaches and assistant coaches in the state. The database was built in Microsoft Excel and analyzed in Microsoft Access.

Gathering the salary and teaching assignment information from 312 public schools proved to be a daily battle. Initially, districts refused to comply or said it would cost hundreds of dollars to produce the information, but eventually we got the data for the salaries for teachers and coaches.

By having the database, we were able to group and total salaries and search quickly for individual information.

Once we had done our analysis and our reporting, we published stories questioning whether education is being compromised for playing football games. We found nearly $80 million in state tax dollars spent for coaches' salaries in 1 year; and head football coaches making 55 percent more than the average for academic teachers.

—Mike Fish, *The Atlanta Journal-*
Constitution

Suggested Exercises

1. Get a database of registered gun dealers from a U.S. state from the Bureau of Tobacco, Alcohol, and Firearms from the from the bureau's website.
2. Do a query searching for a city.
3. Do a query in which you group and count the gun dealers in each city in the state. Sort the records from highest to lowest number of gun dealers.
4. Do a query in which you group and count gun dealers by ZIP code in the city and the largest city in the state. Sort the records from highest to lowest number of gun dealers.

Database Managers, Part 2

7

Matchmaking

> Taking two large databases, one of people licensed to work as aides in home health care and one of criminals, *The Star-Ledger*, based in Newark, New Jersey, found more than 100 recently convicted criminals certified to work unsupervised in the homes of the most vulnerable residents of the state. The matching of criminal identities with aides' identities helped reveal lax state policies and also helped protect those needing assistance at home.
> —Robert Gebeloff, formerly of *The Star-Ledger*, now at *The New York Times*

As you can see from this public-service story, one of most valuable uses of a database manager is matching information in one file to information in another file.

This chapter covers using the relational databases in which tabular files—known as tables—are intentionally joined to one another. As mentioned, information is separated into "linked" tables because it organizes the information and cuts back on the amount of time it takes to do data entry and analysis. But many reporters now use database managers to perform enterprising comparisons of files never created to be linked together—as Robert Gebeloff did in cross-referencing files of licensed health care providers and recently convicted criminals.

For decades, reporters have looked at relationships between people and organizations. In campaign finance, they have tracked businesses' contributions to a candidate and government contracts that those businesses were awarded after the candidate won election.

Other reporters have looked at criminal incidents in the context of local police department decisions on deploying its patrol officers. Others examined environmental agency files on waste dumps and their locations and then looked at U.S. Census information to see whether the dumps were being placed in low-income areas, where the local populace had little political clout.

Utilizing a database manager and relational databases to do these tasks—once done with hard copy records—is the kind of data reporting that is now routinely performed.

Relational Databases Are Everywhere

In the 21st century, information about you is kept in many relational databases. (That's how marketing people find you to make those annoying phone calls, send you spam emails, or barrage you with direct mail.)

If you have a job at a large business or with a government agency, the organization probably manages your paycheck in a relational database. Figure 7.1 illustrates what the record layout in a table that includes your information might look like.

Employee	
Field Name	**Data Type**
EmployeeID	Text
Lastname	Text
Firstname	Text
Street	Text
City	Text
ZIP	Text

Figure 7.1

In another table is a list of the paychecks you received and the date that you received them. Figure 7.2 shows the record layout in this table.

Employee	EmployeePay	
	Field Name	**Data Type**
	EmployeeID	Text
	Pay	Number
	Paydate	Date/Time

Figure 7.2

Note that each table has an employee ID and that only an ID, not a name, appears in the paychecks table. The ID field is known as a key field. It's the field that links the two tables together, as shown in Microsoft Access's Query by Example visualization in Figure 7.3.

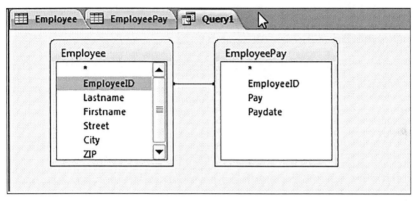

Figure 7.3

As noted in the previous chapter in a relational database, you link tables together using a query. By linking the two tables, an employee's name with payroll information is matched to his or her mailing address. This data structure saves space because you don't have to type address information about the employee each time you enter information about payroll. The tables also organize information efficiently into subjects. Database managers can automatically create key fields of IDs or can use an already existing ID.

What's the most universal key field in the United States? The Social Security number. If you have someone's Social Security number, you can link tables and tables of information together from different databases.

Joining Tables

But how do you create such a link? You tell the database manager that when the *ID number* in a record in the employee table equals the ID number in employee payroll, then the information should be matched, creating a record potentially with all the columns of information in both tables. In Access, you can actually draw a line from one table to another by clicking on the employee ID field and then dragging the cursor onto the employee ID in the salary table, as in Figure 7.3.

But in SQL you could write a "where" statement or "where" or "join" statement in DB Browser. Either statement would link the two files together. SQL helps you think clearly about the questions you are asking and ask them quickly, once SQL is mastered.

Many governmental databases you request will be relational, as shown in Chapter 6. You need to know what government officials mean when they say it's a relational database. You also need to know to ask what the key field is or key fields are.

As you learned in Chapter 6, one of the most used databases in the United States is from the Federal Election Commission (FEC). If you obtain data from the FEC, you will receive a candidates table, a political action committee contribution table, an individual contributor table, and a political committee table. As demonstrated in an abbreviated example in a previous chapter, you can link those tables by the ID numbers of committees and candidates.

To find information about a candidate, you would go to the candidates table. In that table, you would find ID numbers for the committees set up by the candidate to receive and record contributions. To find information about the committees, you would link the candidates table to the political action committee contribution table through the ID numbers. To determine which individuals contributed to the candidate, you would link the committee table to the individual contributor table, again using the committee ID that is present in both tables. It's not unlike building bridges between islands of information, as shown in Chapter 6 in the schema of the hazardous material transportation database and its tables.

For our immediate purposes, we can return to the simplified FEC data we used in Chapter 6. One table contained information on contributors and one contained information on candidates. In this chapter, we will work with the two tables as opposed to one at a time.

To use the two tables in DB Browser, decide on the fields you want to include. In this case, we want to use from the Givers table the last name (last) of the giver, the amount from giver, and the name of the candidate.

So let's do the query to find which givers gave to which candidates and analyze it. Here is the query and the results in Figure 7.4.

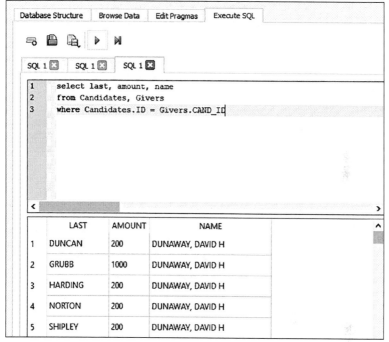

Figure 7.4

Note that the candidate tables, Candidates and Givers, have been brought together. Now that we have correctly linked the tables, we can treat the two tables as one and choose fields from each as though we were at one big buffet table where we can choose fields from either of the two original tables.

Enterprise Matchmaking

The previous example is a case of "intentional" matching or joining of tables. That is, the tables were created with the intent to be joined. But journalists can do extraordinary work by linking tables that weren't created to be linked. In this way, journalists can cross the borders between agencies, professions, and fiefdoms.

For decades, journalists have used **enterprising matchmaking** to ferret out criminals in school systems, nursing homes, or home health-care programs. Other examples include finding out whether lottery sales are primarily in low-income areas and whether legislators who set taxes are actually paying their own. Journalists, responding to allegations of voter fraud, have also sought information on dead citizens on voter registration rolls to link street addresses or names of voters with names on death certificates. The possibilities are limited only by the imagination of the journalist and the availability of the data.

Journalists seldom have others' Social Security numbers, and therefore must be creative in coming up with one or more key fields to link unrelated databases. Several newspapers have discovered criminals working in school classrooms, despite rules that prohibit felons—in particular, child molesters—from being hired for such positions. The most common match has involved linking court or prison records to employee records. This has been done by matching several fields, such as first name to first name, last name to last name, and date of birth to date of birth (if you can get it) or by linking other identifying information such as addresses.

In Figure 7.5, for example, you have criminals. (None of these names represent real people.)

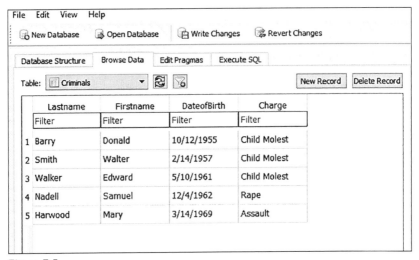

Figure 7.5

In Figure 7.6 you have a table of teachers.

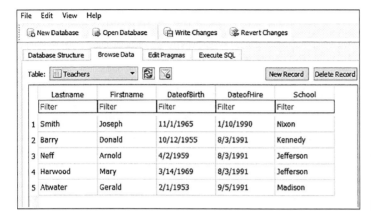

Figure 7.6

Since you don't have a key field, such as a Social Security number, you look at both tables and choose several fields since you don't have a key field such as a Social Security number. To link, you do your inner join statement.

In this case, select the fields Lastname, Firstname, School, and DateofBirth from the Teachers table, and DateofBirth and Charge from the Criminals table.

Run the query and the result would look like Figure 7.7, showing the potential matches between teachers and criminals.

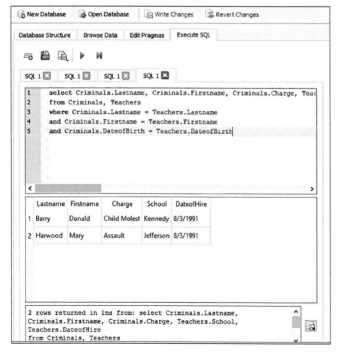

Figure 7.7

Note that field names used to join the tables do not have to be in the select statement. If you want to feel sure about your matches, you can include them in the select statement if you want to.

At this point, however, your reporting would have just begun. You will need to double-check your results, use other documents to verify that any record matches are indeed for the same person, and then prepare to conduct difficult interviews with the employees and the school system officials.

A good number of *matches* (or "**hits**," as they are sometimes known) in such unrelated databases can lead to good public-service journalism that protects the weak or vulnerable. *The Charlotte Observer* in North Carolina produced such a story. In Massachusetts, Brad Goldstein, formerly of *The Eagle-Tribune*, in the city of Lawrence, found welfare recipients in jail by matching the names of recipients with a list of prison inmates. At the *Miami Herald*, Steve Doig matched building inspection records after Hurricane Andrew with wind velocities in the same areas; if the wind velocity was low and the damage was high, then he knew there likely was a problem with construction standards in that area. *The Atlanta Journal-Constitution* discovered that teachers who were convicted felons had escaped scrutiny when being hired. Other reporters have compared parking tickets and weather conditions to show that such tickets are seldom given out when the weather is bad.

It should be noted that the value of matchmaking is limited by the validity of the comparison. You need to be sure of the accuracy of each match and that requires more work including reviewing your own work and then, as mentioned, finding ways through other documents and interviews to ensure the matches are accurate and your story is solid.

Once you use relational databases it becomes possible to handle a more complex one, such as that shown in the visualization (known as a schema) of the relational database of the transportation of hazardous materials in Figure 7.8.

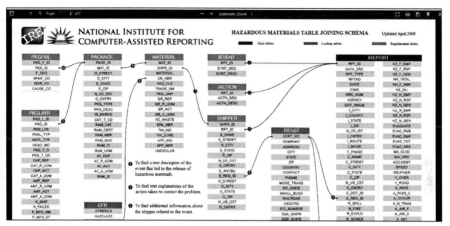

Figure 7.8

This also can provide ideas on how to create more enterprising matches. With this kind of schema in mind I acquired and linked seven different databases on Connecticut state employees through the employee IDs, which were not social security numbers and thus not deemed private.

The database included regular pay, overtime, pensions, and time and attendance. I developed a series of stories as I acquired each database and then more stories as I began doing matches between the databases. In one story, using the regular pay table and the time and attendance table and multiplying hourly pay by the numbers of days off, I showed that, on average, it appeared that one third of the pay to state employees was for time away from the job such vacation, illness, holidays, and workers' compensation.

Chapter Summary

- Database managers allow you to join two or more tables of information by matching names or identification numbers.
- Not only can you join tables intended to be joined, but you can also join those that no one had thought of joining as a basis for enterprising stories.
- SQL is part of most database managers and is a powerful program that can allow you do many queries more simply and powerfully.

Applying CAR

The Dayton Daily News identified 30 cases of neglect by using a database of death cases and a database of group homes for the mentally retarded and documenting drowning or choking of clients, assaults, and other forms of death.

The overall system of homes for the mentally retarded is cloaked in secrecy and difficult to obtain records from. To get around that, we matched the addresses of 400,000 death records with the addresses of dozens of group homes. Using the matches we found in the addresses, we then contacted family members and examined the inspection records of every group home.

We also talked to group home operators, advocates for the mentally retarded, surviving family members, caseworkers, and state and local regulators. Our finding: Ohio's $1.85 billion system to protect 63,000 people with mental retardation is riddled with gaps that have deadly consequences.

As result, the governor appointed a task force and the state auditor was asked to audit private companies under contract to provide care.

—John Erickson, *The Dayton Daily News*

Suggested Exercises

1. Obtain the sample databases of contributions and candidates from the website of this book.
2. Join the tables in the database.
3. Group and sum amounts by last name, by occupation, and then by contribution date. Sort each result by the highest amounts contributed.
4. Repeat the same query using candidate's names.

Part II

Using Computer-
Assisted Reporting
in News Stories

Getting Data Not on the Web

How to Find and Negotiate for Data

New Jersey state officials turned down the Asbury Park Press' request that would help the paper measure the performance of the state's child protection agency. But we learned of federal government databases that contained information on children in foster care throughout the United States, including New Jersey. We also learned of a federal law that required the data to be released and used that knowledge to persuade the state officials to release their data for 2 years.

We succeeded in getting the electronic information necessary to examine the system and produce a 5-day series that showed the state had done little to reform its system and that children were spending more time than ever in foster care and group homes.

—Jason Method, formerly of *Asbury Park Press*

Sometimes, the database you need for a story is openly distributed. Sometimes, however, it is kept from you under the guise of confidentiality or national security, even though it would be easy for officials to remove or restrict access to the sensitive material. Officials also may limit access to data by charging absurdly high prices for it. What this means is that a journalist often may have to dig, argue, and push to get data that should be and could be released readily and for free.

When seeking public information in electronic form, remember that taxpayers have already supplied the money to enter the data, store the data, and retrieve the data. Therefore, you should not have to give the agency a good reason to release it. Instead, the

---

BOX 8.1 Steps for Finding Data

This chapter will look at the three steps—finding, negotiating, and importing—for obtaining access to databases so that you can use them in a story. All three steps go together:

1. You need to *find* the right database or databases for the story and determine what information within it you really need.
2. You often need to *negotiate* knowledgeably for the database, avoid stonewalling by bureaucrats who try to snow you with technical terms, and make sure you acquire any supplementary material necessary to understand the database.
3. You need to know how to *import*, or transfer, the data from a diskette or other source media so that you can use it.

---

keeper of public information should have to give you a good reason *not* to release the information. In short, you need to think, but not necessarily say: "You have it. I want it. Give it to me." A free and democratic society is based on openness, not an obstructive bureaucracy and secrecy, and it is a journalist's duty and prerogative to pursue information.

Finding Data

Many journalists starting out in data journalism wonder where they can find useful databases. The answer, more than ever is "everywhere," no matter where you are in the world. With advent of the web in the 1990s, databases crossing borders and continents increased immensely

We will focus on government databases because many private databases are not only hard to get, but also are priced well beyond the budget of a journalist or newsrooms. In addition, many private and commercial databases are actually stitched together from public databases with the very skills you are learning in this book. Quite often, you can do most of the linking of databases yourself.

There are databases on almost any subject and at almost every governmental agency and business. Since the proliferation of personal computers, such organizations have been storing their information electronically. In addition, they have inventoried and indexed their databases more thoroughly than in the past, especially because of the so-called Y2K concerns prior to the year 2000, when agencies worried that their databases could be reduced to chaos because of date problems on January 1, 2000. Many agencies had used only two digits for years in the 20th century, meaning years "01" and "02" were ambiguous once the 21st century started.

Even without these indexes of databases, you know that most agencies are computerized and have extensive databases. When you walk into an agency, look around and you'll see everyone typing information into computers. If you see a report with tables of columns and rows, there generally is a database behind the report, and you should try to get it if it looks useful for your work. For example, housing agencies often issue reports about where subsidized housing is located, how many units are at that location, and who can qualify for the housing. By asking for the backup database behind those reports, a reporter can obtain not only the columns and rows that appear in the reports, but also material that might have been excluded, such as politically embarrassing information.

It's also good to keep in mind that you may be seeing only a portion of a database when you view it on the web. Even if an era of open government and databases is posted on the web, databases are often only summaries or portions of the original database. It also is common for the original database to have information that officials don't want released or don't realize could be of value to the public. And what is on the web does not always go back for several years.

Although some governments require agencies to provide lists of databases, many governmental agencies may say that a database doesn't exist. This may be because they don't want to be burdened with granting such requests or because they have something to hide.

It is worth investigating whether those same agencies have hired consultants to unravel the mess the agencies made of their computer systems over the past decades. If so, the consultants are likely issued reports, and in those reports can be found inventories of hardware, software, and databases—information that can help you determine whether an agency has what you need. To get this information, ask the agency for copies of consultant reports on its computer systems and databases.

Auditors' reports also generally contain an overview of an agency's records and how they are kept. The Government Accountability Office (www.gao.gov), a congressional watchdog that performs audits of federal agencies, actually uses many agencies' own databases for its audits. In the back of the GAO reports, the databases are described. Although the databases may not be available online, reports, summaries, and discussions of those databases are mentioned.

You can also look through commercial and governmental database catalogs and online directories. In some cases, an agency staff member may be unaware of the agency's databases. In addition, developing source relationships with social scientists at universities and colleges can open up wide avenues of database possibilities. Those social researchers live in a world of databases, because they rely on data for their statistical analyses.

In some cases, administrators and their public information officers may not want to talk to the press or may even mislead reporters. That's why it's good to have sources at all three levels. Also, sometimes the administrators and information officers don't have a clue on what databases exist or what they contain.

There are also associations to know about or join. People who belong to groups that use SAS or SPSS or R (the statistical software packages) or GIS groups (Geographical Information Systems) know about a wide range of data, from hospitals to insurance to government. The Association for Public Data Users (APDU; http://apdu.org/membership/join-apdu/) could be worth joining as an affiliate—but if you can afford it, it's worth it.

BOX 8.2 **Three Levels of Sources**

If you cover a beat, you should develop sources at three levels or more:

1. Talk to data entry clerks who have little involvement in departmental politics; they can tell you what kind of information they are entering.
2. Talk to data processors: they can tell you what kind of information they are processing.
3. Talk to administrators: they can tell you what kind of information they use for the reports they issue.

The APDU puts out a monthly newsletter that discusses various public data. The mapping company ESRI holds an international conference each year in which databases are discussed during their hundreds of sessions.

Obtaining a Database

The first approach to obtaining a database is simply to ask for it. Do not write a formal request under the Freedom of Information Act of your state or country's open records law. You can just ask.

In a time of security-conscious officials, you may be required to write a request. But if getting a database becomes cumbersome or the officials demand a formal request, then you will have to hunker down and do some legwork.

To obtain a database, you need to know what to ask for. You need to know the laws and regulations governing the release of electronic information, though not necessarily to use them as leverage. Sometimes, it is good to know about the rules and regulations so that you *don't* bring them up. Some laws are so antiquated or ambiguous that officials can utilize the laws to effectively block the release of information. To get help on this in the U.S., check the Reporters Committee for Freedom of the Press (www.rcfp.org) for laws and the latest on access to databases in the U.S. The Global Investigative Journalism Network has a good portal to international freedom of information laws at https://gijn.org/resources/freedom-of-information-laws/. The book *The Art of Access* by David Cuillier and Charles Davis is an excellent resource on acquiring public documents and data in the U.S.

Before you begin to battle for information, make sure you know what database you want and what part of it you must have for the story. Conversely, know what you can give up. If you only really need ZIP codes for your story, don't argue over street addresses.

Finally, you need to know how the information is kept. Is it in a spreadsheet or database manager, or even in some ancient programming language? In what kind of format can the agency give the data to you? What does the *record layout* look like? How many records are in the file and how large is the file? How many megabytes or gigabytes are in the file? Answers to these questions tell you what hardware, software, and knowledge you will need if you want to make the best use of the data.

The Record Layout

As noted earlier, a record layout tells you the names of the columns, what types of data are in a column (text, numeric, date), and the width of each column. It's your road map to the structure of the database.

If the information is in a spreadsheet, chances are good that you won't need to know too much. With spreadsheets, you generally get the copy and open the file, and your own spreadsheet program automatically places the information on the spreadsheet grid. You will need to know what the names of the columns mean and get a code sheet in case codes are used. You should also check whether the data type is correct and that numeric columns are not mistakenly in text.

Like downloading data from the internet, that's the easy way to get a database. Frequently, however, you will get information that has been kept in a database manager that you learned about in chapters 6 and 7.

BOX 8.3 Parts of the Record Layout

To understand the information in a database, you will definitely need a record layout. A record layout serves as a guide to how the information is stored and ordered. The record layout specifies:

- The name of each field.
- Whether it's a field that is text, also known as alphanumeric or character (consisting of letters and numbers), numeric (only numbers), or dates.
- How wide each field is. A field can contain only so many characters or numbers, depending on its width. (It's like filling out test forms that give you only 12 spaces for your last name. If your last name is Rumpelstilskin, only "Rumpelstilsk" will fit.)
- The position of the field in the record. If a record is 100 characters long and the last name field is the first field and 12 spaces wide, then the last name field's position is 1 through 12. Think of a record as a linear crossword puzzle.

While width (also known as length) of a field is not as important as in the past, it is still good to know.

The record layout will tell you what information is in the database and whether it fits your needs. You may need some explanation of the categories of information, because sometimes they are abbreviated with acronyms. For example, in the layout for small business administration loan program, you can see there are many fields and some have abbreviations that need explanation. Figure 8.1 shows only about half of the record layout.

	A	B	C
3	BorrName	Borrower name	text
4	BorrStreet	Borrower street address	text
5	BorrCity	Borrower city	text
6	BorrState	Borrower state	text
7	BorrZip	Borrower zip code	text
8	BankName	Name of the bank that the loan is currently assigned to	text
9	BankStreet	Bank street address	text
10	BankCity	Bank city	text
11	BankState	Bank state	text
12	BankZip	Bank zip code	text
13	GrossApproval	Total loan amount	number
14	SBAGuaranteedApproval	Amount of SBA's loan guaranty	number
15	ApprovalDate	Date the loan was approved	date
16	ApprovalFiscalYear	Fiscal year the loan was approved	text
17	DeliveryMethod	Specific delivery method loan was approved under. See SOP 50 10 5 for definitions and rules for each delivery method. 7(a) Delivery Methods: • CA = Community Advantage • CLP = Certified Lenders Program • COMM EXPRS = Community Express (inactive) • DFP = Dealer Floor Plan (inactive) • DIRECT = Direct Loan (inactive) • EWCP = Export Working Capital Program • EXP CO GTY = Co-guaranty with Export-Import Bank (inactive) • EXPRES EXP = Export Express • GO LOANS = Gulf Opportunity Loan (inactive) • INTER TRDE = International Trade • OTH 7A = Other 7(a) Loan • PATRIOT EX = Patriot Express (inactive) • PLP = Preferred Lender Program • RLA = Rural Lender Advantage (inactive) • SBA EXPRES = SBA Express • SLA = Small Loan Advantage • USCAIP = US Community Adjustment and Investment Program • Y2K = Y2K Loan (inactive)	text

Figure 8.1

If codes are used in the data but code information is not included in the record layout, you also should obtain the applicable **codebook** (or code sheet or data dictionary, which means the same thing). This is not programming code, but a document that translates what a code number or letter may actually mean.

Codes are used to save space or to make statistical analysis easier. Let's say a database maker does not want to write out terms for race and ethnicity, such as "black," "white," or "Hispanic." To save time on data entry and space, the database maker would design the applicable column to have only one character. The database maker then codes blacks as "1," whites as "2," and Hispanics as "3." (Number codes allow statistical software to more easily do analysis.) You might be able to figure that out on your own, but you really don't want to get into a guessing game, as this can result in mistaken assumptions. So obtain the codebook or the code sheet. (Sometimes it also is called a data dictionary.)

You should also get a printout of the first 10–100 records to see whether information has been entered into all of the fields. You also need the printout to make sure that you have transferred the information properly into your computer. Also, get a hard copy of the form from which the information was entered. These are known as integrity checks in Chapter 10.

To review, if you are given a database, you need to ask what language the database is in and request a record layout, a code sheet, and, if possible, a printout of the first 100 records.

Privacy and Security Issues

Over the past decade, politicians and the public have become increasingly concerned about privacy and national security. They have denied requests for electronic information even though the same information is available in hard copy or could be collated from publically available sources.

Jennifer LaFleur, a longtime practitioner and trainer in CAR, was once denied access on an Adopt-A-Highway electronic database. Officials said that, under California law, the information on names in the database was private, even though the names are on public billboards where the donors claim credit for the upkeep of that portion of the highway.

In fact, a group of journalists at a seminar in the 1990s came up with 38 excuses that bureaucrats gave for not giving out databases. The same excuses are being used today. You can get the list from the National Institute for Computer-Assisted Reporting (NICAR). Some of those excuses include claims that it will take too much time or the bureaucrat isn't sure how to make a copy of the data.

If an agency claims that its information is private or withheld because of security reasons, you should check the laws and regulations. If the agency is right, you need to decide whether the information you do have access to is still valuable.

Many reporters, by knowing what they need for a story, can agree to the deletion of certain categories. Sometimes you can give up the "name" field because you need the database for a demographic or statistical study. Rather than enter into extended negotiations, consider whether you can give up some fields in exchange for the rest and still get your story.

For instance, reporters often give up names on medical or workers' compensation records because there are a large number of cases in open civil court that can be used for anecdotes. If you are seeking state employee records, you can still do the research for many stories without getting the employees' street addresses.

High Costs

News organizations have been asked to pay millions of dollars when their reporters are seeking information. One time, the database library at NICAR was asked by the U.S. Justice Department to pay more than $2 billion for a database—an absurd amount.

More often, the final cost turns out to be a few hundred dollars or less. Years ago, the state of Connecticut quoted *The Hartford Courant*

BOX 8.4 **Fair Price**

You can prevail on costs if you are willing to haggle and if you know what a fair price should be. Consider the following:

- *The cost of the media.* This should be negligible. A DVD or flash drive costs very little.
- *The cost of copying.* An agency should not charge you for the simple copying of data from a server.
- *The cost of staff time.* Generally, the public has already paid for the collection and storage of data. Unless you ask for special programming, an agency should be hard-pressed to charge you for programming. If it does, the cost should not be more than $20 or $30 an hour.

for a cost of $3 million for access to drivers' license records, when they were still available under the law. Three years later, after extended negotiations, *The Courant* paid a total of $1.

When possible, you should avoid asking for additional programming. It means that errors can be introduced and it gives the agency one more chance to remove records that might lead to an embarrassing story. Sometimes, agencies say that creating a special data set is the equivalent of creating "new" records, and some laws do not require an agency to do that.

In practical terms, you should be able to obtain most databases for free or less than $100. Even in those cases where a fee is stated, you should ask for a fee waiver because the Freedom of Information Act generally calls for the waiver of fees if disclosure of the information is in the public's interest.

One threat to the open use of electronic records is the handling of public records by private vendors. Public agencies that don't have computer expertise often hire commercial vendors to do the work for them. But commercial vendors want to make a profit. If a citizen asks for the information, commercial vendors may be allowed by law to charge high costs for copies of the files. Since some agencies don't have a copy of their own records, you then have to argue with the commercial vendor.

Your best solution is to get your news organization and others to push for changing the law. In some states it is illegal for commercial vendors to charge exorbitant prices for public records.

Importing

You don't want to go through all of the work of obtaining a database and then not be able to use it. That's why you have to be careful to get the record layout, size of the file, code sheet, and printout.

There are two key points when you import data. One, make sure that the information goes into the correct columns and that those columns are labeled correctly. Two, make sure that the information is properly translated so that you can read it. This is a much less frequent problem than it used to be.

If you receive the data in one of the common software programs, your job will be straightforward. Once, databases created in one software program could not be translated into the database software of other companies, but now most of them can. As an example, if you are importing an CSV file into Excel it will be automatically loaded in a spreadsheet To get an idea of the possibilities, just go to open file on Excel and click on the arrow by Excel files and you will see this as shown in Figure 8.2.

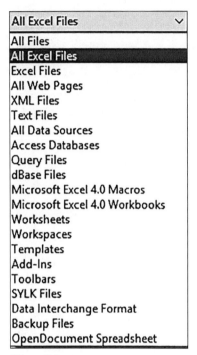

All Excel Files	⌄
All Files	
All Excel Files	
Excel Files	
All Web Pages	
XML Files	
Text Files	
All Data Sources	
Access Databases	
Query Files	
dBase Files	
Microsoft Excel 4.0 Macros	
Microsoft Excel 4.0 Workbooks	
Worksheets	
Workspaces	
Templates	
Add-Ins	
Toolbars	
SYLK Files	
Data Interchange Format	
Backup Files	
OpenDocument Spreadsheet	

Figure 8.2

This is very similar to the import screens we see in Microsoft Excel, but it is even more extensive in Microsoft Access and in some other software. Excel and Access can translate files created with many kinds of software. Other databases, such as DB Browser SQLite, can handle only delimited files or DB files so you would have to convert Excel files into comma delimited.

Sometimes you will receive information in "fixed format" and "comma delimited," both formats used for databases on the web. These formats are discussed in Chapter 2.

The comma delimited format is used to save space. Instead of having blank spaces between columns, the columns are shoved together. Programs know to end a column when they see a comma.

Quotation marks tell the software that the words in between them should go into character fields. The other information is numeric. (In addition, you often can put field names in the first row to save yourself the time of typing them in again and again.)

Fixed format files are a little tricky because sometimes it is necessary to set up a file to catch the information in the proper column, but these are becoming rare. But Excel and database managers often have Wizard just like Excel, and it will lead you through the same steps.

Without the right data, you can't report as accurately and completely on a story. Finding and importing data can be tricky at times, but it's an integral part of CAR. The good news is that the more you do it, the easier it will become.

Chapter Summary

- You can locate databases by looking for computers on your beat or asking where charts and tabulated numbers in reports come from.
- Federal and state agencies are putting more and more of their database listings online, yet at the same time are closing off certain information because of security and privacy concerns.
- Consultants and auditors identify databases in their reports that you might not know about otherwise.
- Always get proper documentation for a database, and always try to get the database for free.
- Know the laws relating to electronic access so that you can use them to your advantage or avoid invoking them.
- Most spreadsheet and database manager software can import most files.

Applying CAR

It took a strong stomach to successfully pull off our "Restaurant Reservations" series, not to mention oodles of computer-assisted reporting resources and considerable tenacity.

We began with several fundamental questions. We wondered whether area restaurants were generally following or failing the rules; whether the government's system of overseeing restaurants was working; and whether the average consumer had any way to distinguish between the safe and unsafe.

Some government agencies resisted our request for inspection data and only relented after official requests, meetings, and follow-up phone calls and emails. Even then, some took weeks or months to provide records. The state Department of Health failed to provide complete data for 6 months and only after we noticed the computer file that it initially provided was incomplete.

Be careful what you ask for, because you just might get it. That's how we felt after the various agencies' data arrived. There were different formats, missing records, duplicate records, and data from ancient computer systems.

But in total we found area restaurants had violated food-safety rules more than 130,000 times over a 5-year period, with 20,000 of those as critical. As for enforcement, we found penalties against violators were rare, even when they were proven to have made people sick.

—Rick Linsk, formerly of the *St. Paul Pioneer Press*

Suggested Exercises

1. Prepare to request electronic information from a local agency for a dataset not on the web, or only partially on the web. Often, agencies do not post all the salaries of their employees. Make a checklist of what you need.
2. Go to the Reporters Committee on Freedom of the Press website (www.rcfp.org) and check out the resources available there.
3. Read your state's open records law. Make notes.
4. Check your state attorney general's website for any opinions relating to your request.
5. Request the record layout and code sheet of the database you seek. Ask to see a printout of some of the records.

6. Be prepared to write an open records request so you are ready if they ask for a written request.
7. Import the data into a spreadsheet or a database manager.
8. Analyze and find out who gets paid the most and what the average and median age is.

Building Your Own Database

How to Develop Exclusive Sources

> We wanted to examine how Swedish authorities attacked financial crime in their country. We built our own database of complaints and suspects from three agencies and by looking through several hundred records built the profile of the average suspect and complaint. We determined that the authorities were not pursuing big time crooks, but instead sitting back and dedicating their time to prosecuting small business owners with bookkeeping trouble.
>
> —Swedish broadcasters Helena Bengtsson and Jenny Nordberg

By building their own database, Bengtsson and Nordberg joined thousands of other reporters throughout the world over the past two decades in learning to effectively create databases for better journalism. Knowing how to build a database is a skill that helps journalists practicing computer-assisted reporting and data journalism because it means they don't have to rely only on databases created by others.

Journalists outside the United States often have significantly less access to data in their countries and find that they need to get paper records and enter information from those records into a spreadsheet or database manager. But U.S. journalists—especially in small towns—have to create databases much more often than you might suppose.

There are many times when the information you want—especially on the local level—is not in a useable electronic form. Furthermore, despite open records laws, recalcitrant officials may not obey those laws. Those officials may delay their responses to requests, cite privacy and security issues to deny access to public data, or set high prices to limit such access.

Consequently, when you can't obtain data in a timely manner, you might have to take up the challenge of building your own databases. Sometimes, the creation of your own database is quick and easy. Sometimes data entry and checking the accuracy of data entry can be time-consuming. To build any database requires some forethought, efficient scheduling, and determination.

But the payoff is well worth it. You will know intimately how accurate the information is. You will start with the database you really need for the story, not a database that will have to be worked with extensively to find what you need. You also can enter the information you want in the most useable format for you. And it provides you with exclusive and frequently powerful stories in which you can report with authority, citing patterns and trends that otherwise would have gone unnoticed. Last, the knowledge of how to build a database makes you a more valuable member of your news organization. Clearly, this is a skill worth having.

Over the past two decades numerous journalists have built their databases on a wide range of international, national, and local issues. Examples include databases on deaths from the terrorist attacks on the World Trade Center, fatalities at race car events, the resale of badly damaged salvage vehicles, questionable pawnshop transactions, employee attendance problems at county agencies and courthouses, sentencing of criminals, the abuse of immigrant workers, and lobbyists' gifts to legislators.

Some journalists build databases to keep track of contacts and sources. Jo Craven McGinty, an expert in CAR and a Pulitzer Prize winner, not only did extensive data analysis on police shootings while at *The Washington Post*, but also kept a database log of contacts with other metropolitan police departments across the United States. When those department officials claimed to forget she had requested information, she could—by referring to her database—cite the date, time, and person she had talked to the last time she called. In many cases, the police officials became more cooperative when confronted with that information.

While at *The Hartford Courant*, I built databases on environmental pollution, lobbyists, campaign finance, and early retirement pensions. However, a database I and two other reporters created on murders possibly involving a serial killer resulted in stories with high impact.

Hearing that police were looking at potential links between two or three murders of women in the Hartford area, I decided to look at newspaper clippings of unsolved murders of women in Connecticut during the past 5 years. There were about 40 cases, and we decided to enter demographic information about the victims in a database manager to see if there were any apparent connections. We included the name of each victim, how she was killed, where she was from, and when her body was found. Not all of the information was available. Still we had enough to work with. We started to filter the information by selecting the town the victim was from.

The town in which a body is found dictates which police department investigates. This means that if a killer disposes of his victims in different towns, then police may be slower to recognize the link between the crimes than if the killer is disposing of the victims in just one town. The local police and medical examiner's office had been investigating the homicides by the town in which each victim *was found*. By looking at the town the victim *was from*, we discovered a clear pattern.

To see that pattern, I ran some simple sorts in a spreadsheet to find out how many of the victims were from the city of Hartford. By looking at the detailed information on these individuals, I found that seven of the women had last been seen in the same neighborhood of Hartford as shown in Figure 9.1.

	A	B	C	D	E	F
1	Lastname	Firstname	AGE	Street	TownFrom	TownFound
2	MAYO	TAMEIKA			HARTFORD	ROCKY HILL
3	TERRY	CARLA			HARTFORD	WINDSOR
4	RIVERA	SANDRA			HARTFORD	SOUTH WINDSOR
5	DANCY	DIEDRE			HARTFORD	HARTFORD
6	PEREZ	EVELYN			HARTFORD	WETHERSFIELD
7	PEEBLES	PATRICIA			HARTFORD	NEWINGTON
8	PARRENO	MARIA			HARTFORD	HARTFORD
9						

Figure 9.1

We looked at further details of the crimes, interviewed family members, and gathered more information from a medical examiner's database and from the FBI supplementary homicide database. We also found two other clusters of murders in the state. As a result of our findings, law enforcement officials formed a task force to study possible connections between all the killings, which until then had not been linked.

Within a year, some law enforcement officials were convinced that not one but three serial killers were operating in the state. Officials arrested one suspect and stepped up their investigations. More important, the Hartford killings stopped.

Other reporters have also created databases for their stories. As mentioned in Chapter 2, Mike Berens, then at *The Columbus Dispatch* in Ohio, created his own database and used similar techniques to track an interstate highway serial killer around the same time as the Hartford killings we were working on. Reporters at *The Seattle Times* also created a database on serial killings in their area. In each of these cases, the database provided tips, illustrated possible patterns, and provided a significant stepping-off point for the journalists. More recently, former data journalist Thomas Hargrove is using national data to identify suspected patterns in communities around the U.S.

When to Build

Anthony DeBarros, who helped create a database on victims of the terrorist attacks at the World Trade Center, said that *USA Today* decided to go forward because the reporters knew at a minimum that a verified list of victims' identities would help with follow-up stories and could provide the basis for enterprise work. Indeed, the newspaper broke stories showing with scrupulous detail how the location of a person's office, along with the building design, affected his or her chance of survival. The database also provided leads on survivors, stories on rescue efforts, and many other stories. It also allowed the newspaper to deal with the confusing and possibly erroneous information that government agencies had about the victims.

"Confronted with such a complex web of facts . . . a database is truly the best tool for unearthing trends that make for compelling stories," DeBarros said.

BOX 9.1 The Checklist for Building a Database

Deciding to build a database should be based on a group of factors. Among them:

- Certainty that the information does not already exist in some kind of electronic form.
- A minimum purpose or a minimum story for which the database can be used, whether it is to keep track of complex information over time or to provide the context for at least one important story.
- Whether the database will be a useful archive and whether reporters can add to it to for future stories.
- How many categories (columns or fields of information) will be required and how many records will have to be entered.
- A realistic estimate regarding the personnel and time needed to create the database.

Once you consider those factors, you can make a well-informed decision about whether to begin.

Spreadsheet or Database Manager

For smaller amounts of information, a spreadsheet is a good tool with which to build a database. A spreadsheet doesn't require first creating a structure in which to enter the data. What you see is what you get. (You can type in the information into a worksheet from smaller data sets, as shown in Chapter 4.)

This means that it is easy to label the columns (or categories) of information, type in the information, and analyze it right away. But if there are many categories of information (more than 20 or 30) and many records (more than few hundred) to be entered, it's worth taking the time to consider working in a database manager.

A database manager is designed to deal with more complex information. It also can streamline data entry by allowing you to use a relational database that enables you to enter basic information once rather than many times. As Chapter 7 shows, data entry of political contributions into two tables meant that the candidates' information did not have to be entered more than one time.

Placing data in a database manager also means you have the option of linking your database to other databases created by government agencies or businesses.

Whether you choose a spreadsheet or database manager, the good news is that once information is in electronic columns and rows it can be easily imported into the other software. Since how to put data into a spreadsheet is pretty self-evident, we will focus on creating a database in a database manager.

Using the Database Manager

Many reporters initially build a database to keep track of information about political contributors. A political database might include the contributor's name, street, city, state, amount given, to whom it was contributed, and date of contribution.

In a spreadsheet or database manager, you need to set up a structure within which to keep the information. This is the same tool known as a *record layout* discussed in Chapter 8. If the information contains words and numbers, you want the type to be in "character" or "text" or "alphanumeric" form.

In the spreadsheet, it's simple matter of deciding on the headers of each column and making sure to format the data type—text, numeric or data.

If it contains numbers that you might want to add, subtract, divide, or multiply, the type should be numeric, also known as numeric. If the information is a date, you want to use the date type; this allows you to calculate the number of days between dates, group by dates, and sort by dates. For example, you might want to see on which dates the most traffic accidents occurred. Or you might want to calculate the actual time served in prison by felons.

Unlike a spreadsheet, where you can type without regard to column width, in a database you may need to think about how many spaces or characters a field will take (just like a crossword puzzle). Most last names can be contained in 25 characters. The codes used for states are always two characters. ZIP codes can be five or nine characters long. Let's look at how you would set up a structure in a database manager. In Microsoft Access, you would open a new database by opening Access, clicking New and Blank database, going to Table Design and finding a grid where you would enter the name of each field and give it a data type. We use Access because it is visually easier to see as in Figure 9.2.

All Access Objects		Table1	CANDIDATES	
Search...			Field Name	Data Type
Tables		ID		Text
CANDIDATES		Candidate		Text
Table1		Party		Text
		Address		Text
		City		Text
		State		Text
		Zipcode		Text
		Year		Text
		District		Text

Figure 9.2

With a database manager, you must be concerned with key areas of the table: the name of the field, the type of data, and the width of the field. (Normally, we would split up the name into at least four fields—last name, first name, middle initial, and suffix—and streets into at least three fields—street number, street name, and street suffix. This ensures that we can sort by any of those fields later.) However, for this example, we will take a shortcut—just like many government agencies do.

Double click on CANDIDATES, and you will go to a screen where you begin typing in data just as you do in a spreadsheet. You can fill the fields in each record in any order that you want to, as in Figure 9.3, and enter entire records in any order you want since a database manager makes data so flexible and easy to sort.

All Access Objects		ID	Candidate	Party	Address	City	State	Zipcode	Year	District
Search...		H203421	SASSER, JAMES REP							
Tables										
CANDIDATES										
Table1										

Figure 9.3

We can replicate this in DB Browser SQLite by making a new database, naming it politics, and it immediately goes to a table where we start typing in field names in Figure 9.4.

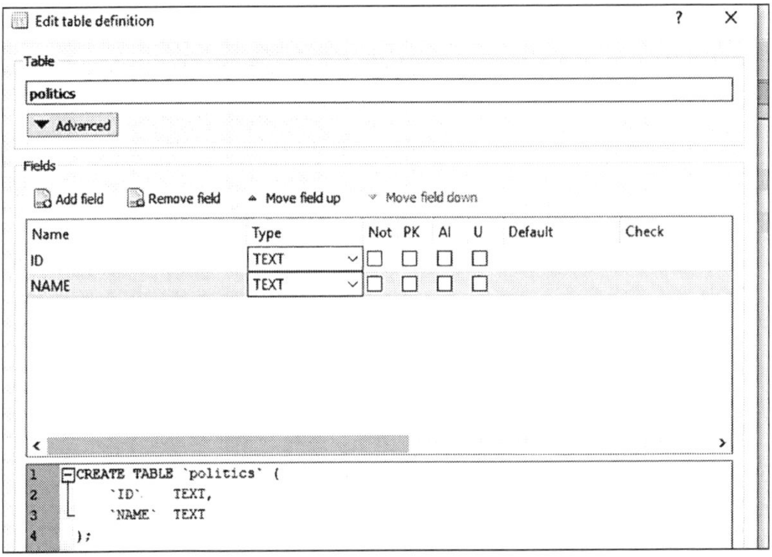

Figure 9.4

As you see, with a little modification and changes in field names, you can create your own database of any information or keep any kind of list of names. You could add dates of birth, ages, or other demographic information such as ethnicity and gender.

Creating a Relational Database

A single table is sometimes called a "flat file" because it doesn't connect with other tables. In the example of campaign finance, however, we know that we want to add another table and link it to the candidates' names through the candidates' ID numbers.

Once again, we click on Create and Table Design. When we come to the grid, we want to type in the field names LASTNAME, REST, CITY, STATE, ZIP, OCCUPATION, CONT_DATE (for contribution date), AMOUNT, and CAND_ID. We use the underscores so that the program sees the field name as one word. (Sometimes, database managers, particularly when using Structured Query Language, have problems with spaces.)

The CAND_ID, as in Chapter 6, is the key field linking the CANDIDATES table to the new table, which we will call the GIVERS table. Figure 9.5 shows what the GIVERS table looks like when completed.

LAST	TEXT
REST	TEXT
CITY	TEXT
STATE	TEXT
ZIP	TEXT
OCCUPATION	TEXT
CONT_DATE	NUMERIC
AMOUNT	INTEGER
CAND_ID	TEXT

Figure 9.5

DB Brower requires another step to make sure that Date/Time differences can be calculated, but Access makes it simple to put in make the data type date.

Most campaign finance laws limit the amount of contributions an individual can make to a single candidate. Let's say, in this example, that you can't give more than $2,000. Microsoft Access also makes it simple to limit the data that can be entered. By typing in <2001 in the Validation Rule line, we can make sure we don't type a number higher than that when doing data entry. (If there is a higher number on a hard copy report from which you are typing, either you have found an error in how someone recorded the contribution or you have uncovered a very interesting story.) Figure 9.6 is an example from Microsoft Access.

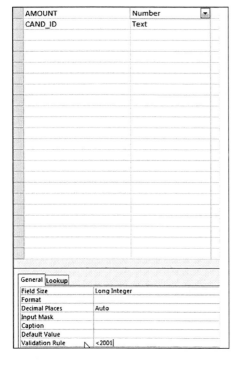

Figure 9.6

Whichever software you use, you now that you have created two tables and you can do all your data entry. By keeping the candidates' ID numbers consistent, you have established a relational database. If you create a new query in your database, you can add the two tables to your query screen and link them through their ID numbers, just as we did in Chapter 7.

These are the basic steps in creating your own database. With a little practice, you will see constant opportunities to create small or large databases for stories. These databases will lead to tips and much better documented stories or just better record keeping.

Chapter Summary

- Spreadsheet and database managers allow you to build your own files of information.
- In building your own tables you can ensure the data is accurate and will serve the needs of your story.
- When building your database, you must plan ahead. You want to ensure that it will have a minimum purpose that will justify the time spent constructing it.
- If you build a good database, it will organize your record keeping, provide tips for stories, and permit you to see and analyze trends and patterns.
- When building a table, always think of possible key fields that will allow you to link the table to other tables.

Applying CAR

River pilots have one of the most dangerous jobs in Louisiana, but we didn't think the issue was as provocative when we first decided to take a look at the people who guide foreign-flagged vessels along the Mississippi River.

At the time, we wanted to find out if two rumors were true: that Louisiana pilots are some of the highest paid mariners in the country and widespread nepotism makes it virtually impossible for non-relatives to join the ranks.

The main records we wanted were their job applications and the accident reports they filled out. We wound up with six boxes of documents, and we took 3 weeks to type everything we needed into Excel spreadsheets.

The results were irrefutable: of the 100 people selected to become river pilots in recent years, 85 were related to other pilots. We further analyzed our own database with both Excel and Access and found serious problems with overall pilot discipline involving lack of punishment and drug abuse.

—Jeffrey Meitrodt, formerly of
The Times-Picayune

Suggested Exercises

1. Using Excel, build a database of your family and friends with their last names, first names, middle initials, street number, street name, street suffix, city, state, ZIP code, phone number, email, dates of birth, sex, and age. Enter at least ten records.
2. Find the average age and median age in your table of family and friends.
3. Using DB Browser, build the same table of your family and friends. Enter at least five records.
4. Find the average age in your table. (Hint: You can find average when you use the Totals line in your queries.)

Dirty Data

How to Fact Check Your Data and Clean It

10

> When the statewide information on Florida designer-drug deaths arrived, it quickly became obvious that the study was riddled with mistakes. In case after case, the victims appeared too young or too old to be designer-drug users. And records showed that it was unlikely that many of the cases had been scrutinized before. Those cases included terminal cancer patients who shot themselves, nursing home patients who fell, and a 4-year-old boy treated for spinal meningitis.
>
> —Hanque Curtis, *The Orlando Sentinel*

Once you start using computer-assisted reporting techniques, it won't be long before you hear and say, "How dirty is the data?" Or to be grammatically correct, how "How dirty *are* the data?"

Dirty data usually begins with key strokes. Remember that it is very possible that someone who was doing one of the most boring jobs (data entry) in the world has entered the information in a database. Or someone has trusted an algorithm with a flaw in the coding to create a database.

Agencies and businesses pay low wages to data entry clerks, which creates and aggravates low morale. Often, an agency is too understaffed to do proper data integrity checks. If the agency does do integrity checks, there is still the possibility of erroneous information not being corrected. Too often, if a program is being used to process data the agency will trust the program to be perfect, which is a very bad idea.

In any case, an agency should put in "validation rules," that is set up an entry system that limits what can be entered into a database. Yet, it is always surprising how typos and errors and just plain wrong information can slip into databases.

Whenever you obtain a new database, always browse through the top 100 records to look for misspellings, omissions and nonsense. You also should run use a pivot table in a spreadsheet or "Group By" query in database manager to see patterns of bad data entry.

For example, if the database contains city names, run a query that asks how many distinct spellings there are and sort alphabetically. (Often the same town is spelled in several different ways.) For example, a U.S. Small Business Administration database on government guaranteed business loans always seems to have errors on names of cities.

If you use a pivot table to count loans in cities in Illinois, you will see many spellings for the same city. In Figure 10.1, the city of Arlington Heights has several different spellings.

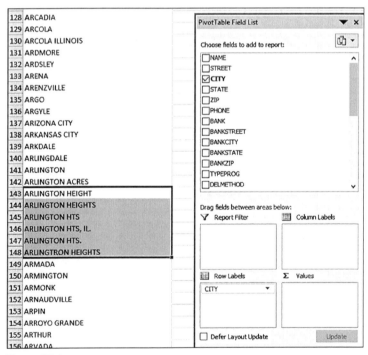

Figure 10.1

[Note that we are using a pivotal table to find the distinct (and dirty) names of cities.]

This prevents you from doing accurate counts and analysis unless you clean the data or do manual calculations. Remember that in computer software, a period or a space and or a hyphen can make the information look different. To a spreadsheet or a database manager, even *St. Louis with a period and St Louis without a period* are different cities.

The lesson is that you must never implicitly trust the data. No database is perfect. No database is complete. Every database is likely to contain a misleading or tricky field. Indeed, George Landau, an early computer-assisted reporting expert, said that all databases are bad databases. You just have to find out how bad they are, what their flaws are, and determine whether they have enough accurate data to be helpful.

For example, the organization EveryBlock, which used local government data to generate online maps, misplaced crimes in Los Angeles by failing to do accuracy checks. The Los Angeles Times did check the data and caused the police department and EveryBlock to make corrections.

The Times did an excellent question and answer with EveryBlock founder, Adrian Holovaty, on the need to check the integrity of data at http://latimesblogs.latimes.com/lanow/2009/04/adrian-holovaty-everyblock.html

Never Trust the Data

Good journalists have always known that they shouldn't trust what anyone tells them until they check the information. (The cliché is that if your mother tells you she loves you, you should check it out.) That same skepticism must be applied to databases. The world is not a perfect place. People are not perfect. If we are working on a story, we try to determine how much one person really knows and then interview another two or three persons to cross-reference and verify what we were told. We should apply these same methods to databases.

Before you begin interviews and go out into the field, you must run these data checks and decide whether you need to clean the data and determine how much of it to clean. Without doing this first, you will be misled just as though a source gave you the wrong tip.

Another good example of problem data was the unintentional trap in a U.S. government contract database that nearly snagged many a journalist and is cautionary tale for any journalist working with data.

The database contained items such as which agency awarded the contract, which company received it, the amount, the year, and the place where work on the contract would be carried out.

Lurking in the database was a field of information called "ObligationType." The field contained one character of information —either "A" or "B"—right after the "dollars" field. [In the layout the "A" means Alphanumeric (any combination of numbers and letters) and "N" means Numeric that will contain numbers that can be put into calculations.] If you did not pay attention to the "obligationtype" field, you could end up with completely erroneous data. Why? Because all the dollar amounts posted in the contract database were positive. If obligation type is "A," the dollar amount remained positive. If obligation type was "B," however, that told you the contract was de-obligated, that is, withdrawn, and the dollar amount should be read as negative. It also meant that you must multiply any dollar amount by –1 if obligation type is "B."

There was no problem if you know to ask what "obligation type" meant or whether the agency that distributed the data told you its meaning, but that was not always the case. In fact, several journalists narrowly dodged a major error in the total value of contracts only because they thought to recheck the database, compare it with paper summary reports, and check back with the agency when they saw hundreds of millions of dollars of difference between their totals and the government reports totals.

BOX 10.1 Lessons Learned

Lessons learned from that other experiences are:

- Pay attention to every field and whether it affects another.
- Do an outer integrity check such as comparing your calculated totals with other's reports.
- Ask questions when the data does not make sense.

Indeed, if they had neglected to multiply dollar amounts by –1 when "obligationtype" was "B," they would have been off by those hundreds of millions of dollars when they did their stories.

BOX 10.2 Kinds of Pitfalls

Dirty databases and shoddy documentation come in many forms. Among the bugaboos:

- Inaccurate record layouts, code sheets, and record counts.
- Typos or a lack of standardization in the spelling of names and places in the database.
- Incomplete data entry.
- Programming characters such as icons or blanks in the data.
- Data with headers because it was copied from a file that was meant to be a printout.
- Inaccurate importing or downloads by the agency or the journalist.

These problems are more common than they should be, but they can be identified and often corrected.

Two Rules

Before we look at these problems and the solutions, there are two rules in dealing with dirty data.

First, never work on the original database. Create a copy of the database and do your work there. If you make a mistake, you want to be able to recover and start again. You can't do that if you changed the original file. Also, as you work with the data, save each major change to the data as a different file, with sequential numbering. This creates an audit trail of your work. For example, working with census data, your first census file might be "states1." The copy would be "states2." The next copy, "states3."

Second, if you need to standardize spellings, never do it in the original field or column. Always create a new field next to it. That way you don't change the original, which can act as a reference point with which you can check your cleaning.

Record Layout

A first step is to review a record layout. From the previous chapters, you know why you need a record layout if you are going to acquire a database. As we have said, the record layout acts as a road map to the database. It tells you the name of the field of information; whether the field contains letters and numbers, just numbers, or dates; and the width of the column, which indicates how many letters or numbers can fit in the particular column.

You also know from a previous chapter that you need the code sheet or codebook that goes with the database. Without the codes, you cannot know that "1" means white or that in another field "4" means felony.

Unfortunately, getting the record layout, the code sheet, and the database is often only the beginning of the struggle to having useable data.

Record Layout Miscues

Many journalists doing computer-assisted reporting have discovered errors in the record layout and the codebook. Moreover, the record layout does not promise that every field has data in it.

For example, for years the FBI annual crime statistics for Chicago did not list rapes because of a disagreement over the definition of rape. The FBI had "0" for rapes in Chicago instead of accepting the city's figures.

State bail and county databases often lack the critical information about whether a defendant *could* post bond and get out of jail. Sometimes the agency has removed, or redacted, the information without saying so.

Let's look at some of the possible problems in record layouts. The sample layout in Figure 10.2 shows how the information might appear within the columns.

Field	Type	Length
First name	Character	15
Last name	Character	20
Agency	Character	20
Salary	Numeric	6

Figure 10.2

In this example, you look at the information before importing it into your database manager. You see the first two records, which are shown in Figure 10.3.

Paul	Jones	Social Services	15541	10/12/2011
Dawn	Brown	Comptroller	21203	05/06/2012

Figure 10.3

Already you notice that something looks wrong. According to Figure 10.3, there should be only four columns of information. But in Figure 10.4 there is an extra column of information that looks like a date. What probably happened is that when the database was first put together, the database designer decided not to include the date of hire. Later, the designer thought the date of hire should be included.

When you are ready to import information into your spreadsheet or your database manager, you may have to set up the structure to hold the information. The database structure generally is a mirror of the record layout as you saw in the last chapter.

But if you imported the information shown in Figure 10.3 into that layout, it would fall into the wrong fields. (This also can happen when trying to convert a PDF file into an Excel file.) The first few records might look like those shown in Figure 10.4.

Firstname	Lastname	Agency	Salary
Paula	Jones	Social Services	15541
10/20/91	Dawn	Brown	Comptroller

Figure 10.4

As you see, in Figure 10.4 the information has shifted and now is falling into the wrong fields. This can often happen when you convert a PDF into an Excel spreadsheet.

A real-life instance of the problem of shifting information happened not to a journalist but to the federal court system in Connecticut.

In Hartford, the court system made use of a voter list to send out notices for jury duty. To get people's names, the court imported a voter registration list into a database it created. Well, Hartford has a large minority population, whereas towns outside Hartford are largely white. Lawyers soon started to notice that the prospective jurors for federal court were mostly white. Eventually, an investigation found that data processors for the court had misread the record layout for voter registration. Instead of allowing eight spaces for the town's name, Hartford, they allowed only seven spaces. Thus, "Hartford" was chopped off at "Hartfor."

The truncation would not have been a problem, except that the following field gave the person's life status. Because the record layout was wrong, the "d" just moved into the next field. In that field, "d" stood for "dead." Of course, the court didn't want to send jury summonses to dead people, so it had created a program that did not include anyone with a status of "d" on its mailing list. To the court's computer, everyone in Hartford was dead. Since no one from Hartford received a jury summons, then there were few people of color on the juries. It made for an excellent story about the government using flawed information without realizing it.

Clearly, it is important to check the record layout against the actual data. It is not uncommon to be given an old record layout or an incomplete one.

Cryptic Codes

Probably more common than a bad record layout is an incomplete or inaccurate code sheet. In the previous chapter, you learned why you need the code sheet or codebook. The codes must be translated or you'll be lost in a forest of numbers. But first you need to make sure the codes are accurate.

Let's say you obtain a code sheet that defines ethnicity by numbers: "1" for white, "2" for black, "3" for Hispanic, "4" for Asian American, and "5" for Native America. Once you have imported the information into your database, you perform a standard integrity check. You run a query or use a pivot table that asks for the number of records for each race. The result is shown in Figure 10.5.

Ethnicity	Totals
1	550
2	430
3	255
4	77
5	88
6	3
7	2
8	1
9	113

Figure 10.5

What's going on? Why are there so few totals for ethnic groups 6, 7, and 8 and why so many for 9? What categories of ethnicity are these. Well, the "6," "7," or "8" could be data entry errors. No one can type hundreds or thousands of numbers without getting a few wrong. After calling the agency, you can probably throw those out. But the "9" cannot be ignored. You call the agency again and learn that they have decided to use "9" when the information wasn't submitted. But they forgot to put that on their code sheet.

In another example, you might be given all the expenditures for every agency in a state. The agencies are listed not by name but by identification numbers, which range from 1001 through 4999. You run a query in which you group the identification numbers and sum the amount column. Figure 10.6 shows what the top of the result might look like:

Agency	Total (in thousands)
1022	255,321
4077	121,444
5019	23,655

Figure 10.6

The result includes an agency identification number, 5019, that does not exist on the code sheet. This can happen more often than expected. For example, many states add and eliminate agencies after the election of a new governor. Often, new identification numbers are added to the database but not to the code sheet. If they are added to a code sheet, they may only be a collection of scribbles on the database administrator's own copy.

Sorry, Wrong Number

The opening discussion of this chapter indicated that it's easy to make mistakes in the millions. You must check to see that all the numbers add up, or at least come close. In the previous chapter you learned 1) to ask how many records you would receive in a database, and 2) to ask for hardcopy reports based on that data.

Again, you also need to do an outer integrity check, which means comparing your analysis to something outside the database such as a written summary report by the agency or an auditor. In the example of the federal contracts database, you would group the agencies and sum the dollars. Then you would compare the sum for each agency with a hardcopy report.

An outer integrity check not only protects against errors, but can lead to excellent news stories. Elliot Jaspin, a pioneer in computer-assisted reporting, performed a simple integrity check when he received a database of low-interest mortgages given out by a state agency to low- and moderate-income people in Rhode Island. Working at *The Providence Journal-Bulletin* at the time, Jaspin totaled the amount of mortgages in the database and compared his figure to the totals published in an annual report. The difference was millions of dollars.

But Jaspin had not made a mistake. Apparently, the agency had been hiding a slush fund, out of which it made loans to the unqualified friends and relatives of politicians. A phone call from Jaspin about the discrepancy worried the agency, which began shredding documents. Soon thereafter the state police raided the agency, and investigations ensued.

Dollar amounts are not the only thing that can go awry. One quick outer integrity check can involve counting the number of records in your database and comparing it with the number the agency said it gave you. If the numbers don't match, you have a serious problem.

However, the situation can be worse. When it is worse, you need to think of all the integrity checks you can do. I once asked for attendance records for 10,000 state employees. The records showed how the employees spent every working hour—whether it was regular time, overtime, sick time, vacation, or personal days. The agency that gave me the records said it had forgotten to do a record count; but because it gave me 1.8 million attendance records, which is what I had counted, I thought I had them all.

However, after a while it occurred to me that I probably should have records for at least 250 days for each employee. Even if an employee left partway through the year, another employee would be earning overtime. A quick calculation of 10,000 employees times 250 days results in 2.5 million records. It took 2 days of debate, but the agency finally looked at its own work, found a serious programming error, and acknowledged that it had shorted me 700,000 records and sent me the 700,000.

Where Is the Standard?

One of the most onerous database problems is the lack of standardization. As mentioned, names can be spelled several different ways or different words used for the same category such as "attorney" or "lawyer" in the Federal Election Commission. It can be time-consuming to fix these problems, but sometimes it's the only way if you want to get accurate counts and summaries.

Let's say go back to the SBA database and fix the Arlington Heights problem. One way to do it is by following the basic concept of cleaning data: you simply use the Excel function of find and replace to make the correction. That way is not only tedious, but you are not making changes in a new column. You would have to work in a new worksheet and then compare back to the original.

A better way to do this is with a lookup worksheet that lists all the wrong spellings with the standardized spelling in the second column, as shown in Figure 10.7.

	A	B	C
1	ARLINGTON HEIGHT	ARLINGTON HEIGHTS	
2	ARLINGTON HEIGHTS	ARLINGTON HEIGHTS	
3	ARLINGTON HTS	ARLINGTON HEIGHTS	
4	ARLINGTON HTS, IL.	ARLINGTON HEIGHTS	
5	ARLINGTON HTS.	ARLINGTON HEIGHTS	
6	ARLINGTRON HEIGHTS	ARLINGTON HEIGHTS	

Figure 10.7

In your original worksheet you create a new column and you put in the VLookup formula in the first cell in the new column that will refer to the lookup worksheet.

When you click, all the wrong spellings of Arlington Heights are corrected as shown in Figure 10.8.

=VLOOKUP(C1,CITYLOOKUP!$A$1:$B$6,2)				
A	B	C	D	E
1 MEINIKE	400 W. NORTHWEST HWY.	ARLINGTON HEIGHT	ARLINGTON HEIGHTS	
2 ANALYTICAL DIRECTIONS, INC.	1509 WOODS DRIVE	ARLINGTON HEIGHTS	ARLINGTON HEIGHTS	
3 CHAPS	1415 W DUNDEE RD	ARLINGTON HEIGHTS	ARLINGTON HEIGHTS	
4 CYBER EXCHANGE	445 E. PALATINE ROAD	ARLINGTON HEIGHTS	ARLINGTON HEIGHTS	
5 A-ARPAD HARDWOOD FLOORING, INC	1312 S EVERGREEN	ARLINGTON HEIGHTS	ARLINGTON HEIGHTS	
6 CREATIVE SALES, INC	762 W. ALGONQUIN ROAD	ARLINGTON HEIGHTS	ARLINGTON HEIGHTS	
7 SOIL & MATERIAL CONSULTANTS,IC	8 W. COLLEGE DRIVE	ARLINGTON HEIGHTS	ARLINGTON HEIGHTS	
8 THE OYSTER REEF,INC.	1744 W. ALGONQUIN RD.	ARLINGTON HEIGHTS	ARLINGTON HEIGHTS	

Figure 10.8

You can see the formula refers to C1 in the original worksheet, the lookup worksheet, which has been named CITYLOOKUP, and then the range of data in CITYLOOKUP, which is two columns and six rows, has been identified.

Another fast, reliable way this can be done is with the Update command in SQL in the DB Browser database manager.

First, you need to create a new field, called Newcity, in Sbaloansillinoisbank.

You do that with just two lines using the "Alter" and "Where" statements as shown Figure 10.9.

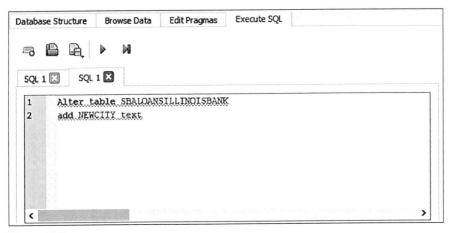

Figure 10.9

Then you fill that field with the correct spelling of Arlington Heights by using a statement that "sets" the correct spelling and uses the where statement to list the misspellings in Figure 10.10.

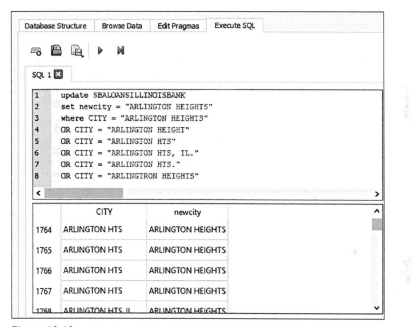

Figure 10.10

Your result is very similar to Excel's VLOOKUP.

Now, if you wanted to count all the loans in Arlington Heights, you could write a query that used Newcity and counted the number of loans and you would get the correct number this time.

This is only the beginning of data cleaning, but the practice of creating a new field and then putting a standardized spelling in that field is common practice and necessary.

Header-Aches

You finally persuade an agency to give you information in an electronic form rather than on a printout. You get the record layout and a DVD or they put in a drop box online for you. You get the data, open it up in your computer, and browse through the information and what do you see? A horror show of headers.

Headers are the bits of information that go across the top of a printout page. They may tell you the date, page number, and other information that has no place in your database of columns and rows. An example is given in Figure 10.11.

Date 0/2/2013	Administrative	Services Page 3	
Name	Town	Zip	Salary
Sun, Gerald	Lincoln	06320	35,004
Moon, Mary	Jefferson	93914	42,523

Figure 10.11

In response, the agency—through incompetence, laziness, or nastiness—apparently gave you the image of each printed-out page instead of the raw data. Fortunately, you can correct the problem with a Word or database manager or a quick program. (We won't go through every step in this handbook, but we'll go over the basic idea of what you can do.)

If you can import the information into a database, you will likely end up with nonsense records at the beginning of each row that starts with "date." For example, the information might look like what you see in Figure 10.11.

But with a "where" statement—such as "delete all records where name like 'Date*' "—you can locate the offending records and eliminate them. In DBrowser you would do a query as you did in updating a table but use % for the wildcard. Then you would follow the same process as updating a table with your query that looked like Figure 10.12.

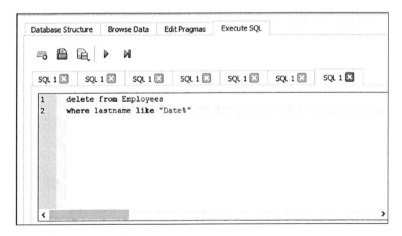

Figure 10.12

Numbers Versus Text

Importing databases incorrectly can lead to cutting off the 0s at the beginning of numbers. But when you import that you may face enormous problems. For example, if a spreadsheet or database manager imports the ZIP code or an identification number into the numeric field, this will cause significant damage. If the database manager sees a ZIP code that begins with a "0," it will eliminate the ZIP code because it looks meaningless.

Thus, for journalists who work in ZIP codes that begin with "0" (such as 01776), all ZIP codes will be entered as four characters (1776) instead of five if the format of the cell or field in numerica Those ZIP codes will be useless not only for mailing addresses but also for matching one database to another.

The same problem can happen with identification codes. An employee with the identification number 042325 will have it rendered as 42325 if it is put into a numeric field. This is inaccurate and also prevents accurate matches.

The way to escape this peril is to always import ZIP codes, identification numbers, and phone numbers into character or text fields. Generally, import as a character field any number that will never be added, subtracted, multiplied or divided. The spreadsheet or database manager then will preserve all the digits.

Fields that contain dates can be another problem. Journalists either pay attention to the format—U.S. (month first) or European format (day first)—and make sure to import it correctly. Sometimes they split the field into three fields (year, month, and day) to make things simpler. Others import the dates into character fields.

Dealing with this problem involves two strategies you already have encountered.

Offensive Characters

Databases can contain offensive characters. They may be weird-looking smiling faces or misplaced commas or semicolons. Before importing information into a database, you probably want to get rid of them. Most programs allow you to do this fairly easily.

Microsoft Word will allow you to click on Find and Replace under the Edit button to basically write a "search and replace" instruction. Say you want to eliminate commas in the data. You would type the comma—,—in the Find part of the box and leave Replace blank. You then click on "Replace All."

There is a fancier way to do this with coding, but you also have a lot of tools in Excel or programming code. **Parsing** has long been a popular way of doing data cleaning in spreadsheets. *Parsing* means drawing column lines between different kinds of data.

The import wizard you saw in Chapter 2 will look at a text file when you open it and suggest column lines. If the text file is in a tabular format (i.e., it looks like columns), the spreadsheet can rapidly arrange the data. This is especially handy for small files downloaded from online. The spreadsheet enables you to do that easily. You can draw lines between the text columns by clicking. You can delete them by putting the cursor on the line and double-clicking. Once again, no database is perfect or complete; but that doesn't mean it cannot be made usable.

In Excel split a field based on a comma or space in the middle of a field. This can be handy when you are trying to match names in one table with names in another. One table may put the first name in a separate field and the last name in another field. But another table may put the last and first name in the same field, such as "Smith, John." To make the names in the second field useful for a match, you can use the comma as a marker to split the name into a first name and a last name in Excel.

This guide does not cover coding, but the National Institute for Computer-Assisted Reporting has many handouts on this and programs that can clean data such as Open Refine and Python. What's important is that you know this kind of data cleaning is possible.

Chapter Summary

- Make sure that identification and ZIP codes contain all numbers.
- Watch for missing words.
- Match the record layout carefully to the actual data.
- Use word processors or string functions in database managers to correct errors.
- Know how many records are supposed to be in the database.
- Use a spreadsheet parsing when the number of records is small.
- Compare total amounts in your database to hardcopy reports.

Applying CAR

The Washington Post series, "Deadly Force," which won a Pulitzer Prize, resulted from a close examination of the FBI's Supplementary Homicide Report. The examination revealed that the SHR data for the country that year did not have a single "81"—the code for a justifiable homicide by a police officer. Neither did any of the other years I checked.

This suggested that whole records were missing from the dataset. The FBI's own documentation provided another corroborating clue. By comparing the number of records cited on the documentation and the number of records in the database, it was clear that there were 287 fewer records than there were supposed to be.

After conversations with the FBI, I found that they did collect the data but did not make it part of their "standard release." After two requests, the FBI delivered another computer tape that contained hundreds of "81s." The raw numbers were remarkable. Only officers in a handful of cities—all much larger than Washington D.C.—had shot and killed more people. Ultimately, these records served as a starting point for the series.

—Jo Craven McGinty, formerly of
The Washington Post, now at
The New York Times

Suggested Exercises

1. Get part of the Federal Election Commission contributor database or use the database Tenncands.
2. Open your table or the use the table Givers. Copy it as new table called Givers2 Create a new field called "occupation2."
3. Copy all the occupations in the occupation field into the occupation2 field.
4. Using the update command, change all attorneys and lawyers in occupation2 to lawyers. Then change all doctors and physicians into doctors.
5. Using occupation2, now group by occupations and total the amounts of contribution.

Doing the Data Journalism and Computer-Assisted Reporting Story

How to Report and Write with Data

> Computer-assisted reporting is no different than other journalism in an important way: often the best stories start with a reporter's gut instinct.
>
> —David Knox, formerly of *The Akron Beacon-Journal*

You have the computer, software, and the understanding that the judicious and skillful use of computer-assisted reporting (CAR) techniques can create good news stories. But now what?

If you're not careful, you can suffer a severe case of reporter's block, trying to figure out what stories to write and how to do them. Worse, a large database can swallow you up with its complexities, distracting you from finishing any story. Instead, stop and consider what you have learned in this book.

CAR is not meant to be a separate endeavor, but rather an integral part of the newsgathering process—interviews, observations, and documents. This ever-increasing part of journalism offers techniques to use, improve and enhance your current reporting, not necessarily take center stage.

Perhaps, most important is the challenge that goes with all stories. What is the larger question you are seeking to answer with this news story, and will the data help answer that question? You can deal with all of these factors with a few key strategies.

BOX 11.1 **Building Your Own Databases Over Time**

Above all, CAR should apply to topics that you are interested in writing about. When you consider using a database or databases for a story, you should contemplate these questions as you learned them in the previous chapters:

- Are there databases relevant to the story that would help with depth, context, or ideas?
- Have you checked online news stories on databanks such as LexisNexis or the Investigative Reporters and Editors (IRE) Resource Center or the Global Investigative Journalism Network to see if anyone used a database for this kind of story?
- Are the databases available on the web? Can they be analyzed on the web or downloaded in useable formats?
- Which software would be appropriate for analyzing the database? A spreadsheet or a database manager? A visualization tool like Tableau?
- Is the database composed of more than one file?
- If the database is not easily available from a website, who keeps the database? What are the open records laws that govern its use? What is the agency's or entity's history when it comes to releasing data?
- How could the database be used graphically? Bar charts? Interactive maps? Other visualizations?
- Who are the people that you will need to profile and interview for this story so that it is not a "dry data" story?
- Will you be able to get out into the field and make observations and compare your observations with the data?
- How do you ensure that the story will be fair and not distort or misrepresent the statistics and data that you use?

Pick a Story You Know Can Be Done

Review stories that have been done at other news organizations and see whether you can apply their approaches and acquire similar databases to illuminate issues in your area. The resource centers at IRE have thousands of data stories indexed at its website, and the Global Investigative Journalism Network also keeps track of international stories.

Many of those stories at IRE, both U.S. and international, have been entered into the IRE awards contest which requires journalists to fill detailed contest forms that explain how they did the story, what databases and documents they used, and what challenges they faced. Those contest entries have been scanned by IRE and you can download and review them.

Pick a Database You Can Get

Quite often, journalists spend most of their time acquiring, cleaning, or building a database when doing a data story. To avoid that time-consuming process, look into obtaining a database that has been released before or get a federal database that can be sliced down to the local level.

The National Institute for Computer-Assisted Reporting (NICAR; www.nicar.org) and ProPublica.org both have data libraries from which data can be extracted for your geographic area or your specific interest. The U.S., Data.gov offers a multitude of databases to download. Some of those databases are useful for any country, but you also can search for data for websites maintained by your own country or you can download data for your country or region from international websites such the World Health Organization, the World Bank, or the United Nations.

If you are going to build a database, follow the guidelines in Chapter 9 to avoid getting bogged down in data entry. When you first start out on a data story, it is advisable to keep your first self-built database small and manageable.

Some First-Time Examples

If you want to look at the first stories some reporters did after they learned these techniques, you can check the "first ventures" reported in Uplink, an IRE blog that is no longer updated but has excellent archive.

- Jason Callicoat of *The South Bend Tribune* in Indiana took weather data and parking ticket data for his first try at a data story. He ended up with two stories. Not only did he discover that residents weren't as likely to get a ticket on a bad weather day, but also that armed forces recruiters owed the city thousands of dollars.

- Edward L. Carter at the *Deseret News* in Utah produced a story illustrating the lack of females in top management positions in local government after getting public data on municipal employees, their salaries, and other employment information.
- Mark Houser of the *Pittsburgh Tribune-Review* used Excel worksheets on lottery sales to help report on high sales to working-class families and other social consequences of Pennsylvania's lottery system.
- Missouri School of Journalism student Mark Greenblatt won an IRE award for using a federal database on the conditions of bridges in Missouri to help him identify deficient and unsafe bridges.
- University of Illinois journalism student Janelle O'Dea gathered fire safety inspections of fraternities and sororities and found repeated dangerous violation.

Start Small

It sometimes is a matter of pride for some journalists to use a database composed of hundreds of thousands or millions of records. But for many journalists, some of the most effective stories have come from only a few hundred or a few thousand records.

Furthermore, starting with a small database allows you to get to know the information in detail. Look for databases that involve only a few columns of names or numbers. Then, if you really have to, or want to, you can manually spot-check the database; doing so will improve your confidence in the information and in your skills.

In the 1980s and early 1990s, most databases came from mainframe computer tapes. They had to be downloaded and broken up into smaller parts to be used on personal computers. Now, laptops can handle enormous databases that can be downloaded. Or you can just put your criteria—city and state, for example—in an online form to download only the information you need.

Some large databases, such as census files, are already broken into small databases in Excel or CSV. Journalists can now routinely use small census files for stories on housing, income, transportation, or ethnic diversity in cities.

Building Your Own

As shown in Chapter 10, it's not that difficult to build your own database. If you do, you immediately take three steps toward a successful story.

1. You automatically are familiar with the information because you obtained and organized the data.
2. Because data entry is so tedious, you will limit the amount of information and keep it relevant.
3. If *you* build a database, then no one else has it, and you may uncover an exclusive story. Remember that a database doesn't have to have thousands or even hundreds of records. Two of the most useful databases I built had fewer than 150 records each.

Journalists Karl Idsvoog and Corky Johnson set a standard in the early 1990s when they showed the effectiveness of building a database. Their databases resulted in sharp investigative stories, including articles on the sale of salvaged cars at a county office, and wasteful practices at a local housing agency.

At *The Hartford Courant*, environmental writer Daniel Jones, researcher Leah Segal, and I built an abbreviated database on emissions of toxic chemicals by manufacturers. (This was after we learned that we would have to wait 9 months for government officials to release their database.) By doing so, we learned a great deal about how companies filled out the hard copy reports, and we learned that the state had not mentioned 20 percent of the emissions in its reports because of administrative decisions. For months, no one else had comparable information, and we used the database for several exclusive stories.

Match the Database to Your Knowledge

Although electronic databases permit you to learn and explore new subjects, it's better to get a database on something you know about when you are starting. Building your own database is one way to be sure of the information and how to use it; getting a database on a topic you know about and cover is another way.

A database is a mirror of reality, but a mirror always has flaws. You need to know how flawed the mirror is and how distorted the image. That's why it's good to get a database about your own beat or specialty, and there are numerous databases available online and offline on just about every beat. The database can highlight problems or provide tips about the subject, but you know the context.

If you find flaws in the database, you have to decide whether it is worth cleaning up those flaws and how long that will take. Some databases simply can't be used without some cleanup, and you need to make an assessment of the time and effort that will take before embarking on such a task. If it is a matter of standardizing a location name, then it will be easy to do. If it's matter of parsing one column into three columns it may take more time. But, again, it can be done pretty quickly.

If you aren't reporting on a familiar subject, then team up with a reporter who does know it. When I worked on a judicial story, I worked with the court reporter. On other subjects, I worked with the environmental reporter, the medical reporter, the city hall reporters, or the political reporters. They pointed out problems in the databases and could also discern patterns and clues in the data.

The Minimum Story

When you are starting out, never get a database without thinking about the minimum story. By "minimum story," I mean the surest, most basic story available. This approach, introduced by legendary investigative editor Robert W. Greene, has been used and taught by veteran journalists for all kinds of reporting.

If you get a database of governmental salaries, you can be pretty sure that you will have a story about the average, the median, and who gets the highest and lowest salaries. If you get a database of housing prices over a span of years, you can be confident that you will have a story about changes and trends. If you get a database on crime, you will undoubtedly be able to report on increases and decreases. If you get a database on political contributions, you will have a story based on who gave the least and most, and where the contributors were from.

These are minimum stories. They don't always become the lead story of the day, but they are solid and enable you to engage in meaningful journalism. They also provide you with a foundation of databases that bolster later stories or can be combined with new databases for even better stories. In addition, they show potential sources that you are interested in the topic.

Keep Up with Other Reporters' Work

Too many journalists get caught up in the argument that a story has been done before. Frankly, many stories have been done before. That's not the point. The real questions are whether your story is a good one, whether the previous stories have been done thoroughly and correctly, and whether your material is of current interest in the geographic area in which you work, and whether it builds on previous similar stories. Some of the examples cited earlier are always interesting such as stories about salaries, inspections, and parking tickets.

The same applies to using databases. After all, a reporter in one community can do a reasonably good overview of who sells guns in that community. Possibly, there is no shattering news, just an interesting look at the issue. But you may get the same database for your own community and discover that many gun dealers are police officers, and that some of them sell guns to convicted felons. It's the quality of the database and what you do with it that counts.

Therefore, it is important to try to keep up with what other journalists are doing. When you read or hear about a journalist who has used a database or online resources that you may be interested in, review the stories to determine how the sources might be applicable in your own situation. You also can call or email the journalist for tips on the database.

NICAR and the Global Investigative Journalism Network offer many resources revealing how journalists have researched data stories and what databases and software were used. There is the NICAR listserv, NICAR-L; and *The IRE Journal*; Nonprofit investigative reporting newsrooms such as Pro Publica (www.ProPublica. org) and *The Guardian* also will explain how they used data for a story.

Integrate Databases into Your Daily Work

Although some journalists use databases only for long projects, you should try to integrate their use into stories on the beat and on the deadline. Indeed, Pat Stith, an inspiring investigative reporter who was a long-time investigative reporter at *The Raleigh News & Observer* and a pioneer in CAR, gave a good tip when he said, "We are going to use databases to create or improve everyday front page stories."

The "improve" part of that statement is especially useful for a journalist beginning to explore CAR. Quietly improve your stories by adding online searches, small spreadsheet calculations, and **summary data** from database managers. You will bring depth and context to your daily and beat reporting that will make every story more important and more informative.

Find a Partner

If at all possible, find a partner to learn with. With any new way of thinking and looking at information, it helps to have someone to talk to and discuss solutions to problems. The "buddy system" keeps you focused and also helps prevent errors. Having a friendly colleague look over your shoulder when you are doing your first queries or calculations will save you a great deal of time and trouble. You will also learn faster by helping someone else.

Become Familiar with the Field of Data Programming

Because you are learning a new subject, take the time to read articles and books about computer hardware, software, databases, and programming language. They can help you learn the lingo and find tools that might help you do a better job.

You should also get to know people who work in programming but who are not journalists or just entering the field. They often have a quick answer for a problem that has baffled you and other journalists. An excellent group to become a part—in addition to NICAR—is Hacks/Hackers (the name short for "journalists and programmers") https://hackshackers.com/. They hold "meetups" that allow for faster exchange of information. Forums on software, social research methods, and public databases also are full of helpful how-to tips and story ideas.

Look for Tips

Keep a narrow focus when you start doing these kinds of stories, but don't overlook potentially good stories or tips in databases.

When you have finished your minimum story, set aside half an hour to go back and peruse a database. (Make that a firm half hour by using a timer, or you could pass half a day or night without realizing it.)

Look for tips by searching for particular words, looking for "outliers," creating summary data using "group by," calculating percentages, or just scanning the databases for trends and patterns. Often, a good story can emerge from such a scan of a database.

Writing the Story

Too often, when starting to write the story, reporters let themselves become overwhelmed by the statistics and numbers. You can't write your notebook, as has often been said.

Throughout the reporting process, especially when dealing with data, numbers, and statistics, you will need to think about summarizing. As Sarah Cohen of *The New York Times* has urged, consider these questions: Which is the one most important number that is central to the story? Is it a raw number like 5,000? Is it a rate, ratio, or percentage increase?

If possible, the key number should be the only number in the first few paragraphs of a story. Most likely, you will have other numbers, but many of them should be visualized in a chart, graph, or map. Otherwise, the reader or viewer will be overwhelmed. If you think it will provide a service, you also can list all of the numbers on a website in a separate file.

Once you have the central number, what is the best human example you have? If you lead a story with an anecdote about one case, it should represent the pattern or outliers you found in the data.

Sometimes, in complex stories, you need to explain how you researched the story and what data you used. Separate from the main story, you can provide details on methodology and data, giving your story more credibility. You also can make the entire database available online so that others can review your work or look for other stories or comment on your work.

In addition, you need to get out and see what you are writing about. If it is toxic dumps, then go look at them. If it is schools, then visit them. If it is small businesses, go there and do interviews. If you do the data work, it is key that you also do the necessary fieldwork and the legwork. And remember that good stories are about people and for people.

Good Reporting and Ethics

Throughout your newsgathering and data work, remember to be accurate and fair. There are plenty of politicians, researchers, and advocates who will want badly to use and publicize numbers that will back up their positions. As an independent journalist, it is your job not only to expose their manipulation of numbers, but also to prevent yourself from seeing the numbers you hope to see.

Quite often, the story turns out to be even a better one if the database doesn't support your initial hypothesis. Either way, the only good story is one that summarizes accurately what you have found.

As you compose your story, you need to be willing to share the highlights of your findings during your interviews and to listen to, and consider, contrasting opinions. In addition, keep an eye out for "lurking variables"—that is, additional factors that could potentially distort the meaning of data. It is much better to find out that you are wrong before you publish a story than after the public sees it.

Throughout our story on racial disparity in how bail amounts were set, court reporter Jack Ewing and I constantly tried to play "devil's advocate" with the data and to come up with arguments against our initial findings. Push your editor or colleagues to help you look at your work critically.

Finally, when the story is complete, go back and recheck your facts line by line. Whenever possible, tie facts back to your data and documents and footnote them as appropriate. And always provide source full information for online or published sources.

Stay Curious, Get Excited

Stay curious and excited about your stories. The lasting attraction of data is that you can do stories you never could have done before in ways you never thought of. Moreover, you can be creative and responsible at the same time and provide the public with the best and most accurate view of an issue.

BOX 11.2 **Reporting with CAR**

Here is a summary of the steps in doing CAR stories:

I. Begin the story with a hypothesis or question.

   A. You get a tip from a person or other source.

   B. Group and sort data you already have to show possible trends, patterns, or unusual events.

   C. You observe an event or condition in your community.

II. Draw up a list of persons to interview, places to visit, and databases and documents to analyze.

   A. People can include experts, agencies, community members, and the custodians and users of relevant data.

   B. Places include agencies, businesses, neighborhoods, or sites to which the data refers.

   C. Databases are those that already are created or those you may have to build from documents or observations. You will need the right software to work with either existing or newly created databases.

III. Prioritize your list and compose a schedule for completing the list.

   A. All open records requests should be made as early as possible.

   B. Plan to interview certain people—usually administrators—at the beginning of your work if you can, after your first run though the data. (You may need to interview the same people after your site visits, further data analysis, and other interviews—see below.)

   C. Do the data analysis again after the interviews. Look for flaws in the data and your methods.

   D. You may need to do your site visits before the data analysis and after the data analysis. Data analysis will help you focus.

   E. You need to take into account that your list of interviews, site visits, and datasets may grow, and you likely will need to re-do your schedule.

IV. Write the story.

   A. Summarize your data work and decide what the key numbers are and what should be visualized in charts or maps.

   B. Summarize your interviews and site visits. Decide who and what are most representative of your reporting and data analysis results.

continued

C. Check your data findings against outside reports based on the data and run your findings past experts or persons familiar with the data.
D. Outline the story and decide on the appropriate tone.
E. Be prepared to re-interview some people and to redo your data analysis as part of the verification process.
F. Write the story.
G. Do a line-by-line check of all of the facts in your story. Use footnotes if that helps.
H. Be prepared to defend your methodology.
I. Plan possible follow-up stories before you publish or air the story.

Chapter Summary

- Focus on databases relating to subjects you know.
- Identify existing and available databases that are useful for your story.
- Build your own database as needed. If new to CAR, start small.
- Look at how other CAR stories were done. (Hint: IRE, NICAR, GIJN, and other sources share information on data stories and how they were done.)
- Use the buddy system—a colleague's viewpoint can make all the difference.
- Use databases as "tipsters," like people who tip you off to good stories or wrongdoing.
- Integrate CAR into your daily journalism.

Applying CAR

After taking a NICAR boot camp, it wasn't long before I was finding ways to use my newfound skill.

In fact, CAR has become an everyday method for me. When I'm looking for information among the first things I ask is how are the records kept? or how far back do those records date? The whole process is always an adventure.

For one story, an initial tip on missing school equipment came from a source in the fixed assets department.

We then requested from the school an inventory of missing equipment.

They declined to give it to us electronically and instead supplied the list on paper. The list totaled $2.5 million of equipment lost over a 5-year period. I entered all the information on an Excel spreadsheet, added up the totals, calculated percentage increase/loss over time, sorted the data to see which schools were losing the most, and looked at the items that were lost the most frequently. The list included *VCRs*, computers, televisions, and band equipment. Two of the most unusual items were a John Deere tractor and a walk-in freezer. Our story created quite a stir and a subsequent audit by the school district revealed that the problem was even worse than we reported: $4.2 million in equipment was missing!

—Joe Ellis, KMOL-TV

Suggested Exercises

1. Research the IRE Resource Center (www.ire.org/resourcecenter) for data stories that have been done.
2. Read journalists' articles, contest entries, or tip sheets kept at IRE to learn about how other journalists used data for their stories. Also, browse the resources at the Global Investigative Journalism Network and the Data Driven Journalism Center, run by the European Journalism Centre http://datadrivenjournalism.net/about.
3. Download three Excel worksheets from the U.S. Census Bureau that have information on topics you are interested in or from the World Bank.

Appendix A
A Short Introduction to Mapping Data

Mapping data is basically taking columns and rows of information and overlaying that information over geographical maps. By doing this well, you can quickly visualize for yourself and readers and viewers what the data means.

For example, using mapping software you can place dots that represent the location of auto accidents on a map of streets and suddenly a list of accidents turns into clusters of dots at certain intersections and you see where the dangerous intersections are.

In this appendix, we look at the basic uses of mapping software—known as Geographical Information Systems (GIS)—and some of the techniques you can employ to visualize your data.

There is now a constant stream of mapping examples in journalism because the mapping of data has quickly evolved from the occasional to routine. It has greatly helped that it has become easier to upload or import columns and rows into GIS software online or on your computer.

Journalists also have several different kinds of software available to them. These include the popular Google Fusion Tables or Google Maps, Tableau, QGIS, and longstanding ESRI products such as Arc Online and its Microsoft add-on known as ESRI Maps.

In addition, more websites, especially government sites, allow you to do mapping on their sites by providing both the data and the mapping software.

With all the options and ease of use, reporters throughout the world have created maps to reveal patterns of drunken driving, property and violent crime, bank and insurance discrimination, landslides, migration, environmental hazards, lottery sales, school test scores, blighted buildings, health problems, white flight, and bad bridges and dams.

Overall, mapping has been done by journalists for more than three decades. Journalists first began making revealing displays of data more frequently in the 1990s. When Hurricane Andrew hit Florida in 1992 the damage was enormous and costly. In its aftermath, *Miami Herald* computer-assisted reporter Steve Doig created a map that overlaid wind speed reports over 60,000 building inspection damage reports. The visual result was stunning.

A reporter would expect to find the areas that experienced high winds speeds would have a large amount of building damage and the areas with lower wind speeds have less damage. But Doig's map showed that some areas with lower wind speeds had high damage. The map tipped off Doig and other *Herald* reporters where to start their investigation into poor building and inspection practices, particularly those done after 1980, and that work led to an expose of incompetence and corruption that won the *Herald* a Pulitzer Prize.

In mapping, data on a topic such as wind speeds is imported into the software and—as in a database manager—key fields in the table on wind speeds such as longitude and latitude are matched to longitude and latitude in a template table.

"Mapping is just such a quick and useful way of taking what could be an otherwise unintelligible pile of information and finding the patterns in it," Doig said.

Doig's and other's ventures inspired thousands of stories throughout the world that have used the power of mapping.

In 2011, *The Guardian* in the United Kingdom did a series of powerful maps on rioting that had broken out in cities in the United Kingdom, one that overlaid suspected rioters addresses and poverty data as shown in Figure A.1.

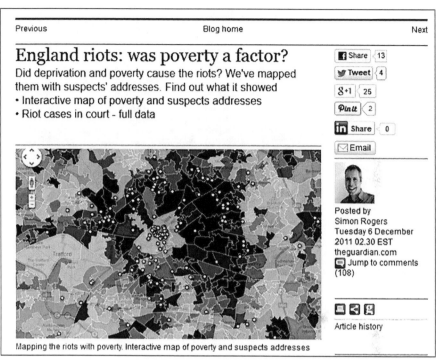

Figure A.1

Turning Matching Sideways

The major concept in mapping is the same one you encounter in database managers: matching. In Chapter 7, we represented matching with the visual interface in Microsoft Access. With mapping software, you think of putting one layer of data on top of another, instead of drawing lines between fields.

But, as is appropriate with mapping, let's illustrate how to do it.

In the first example, we will use a Google Fusion Table to looks at local dataset of fires.

The dataset of building fires in the city of Champaign, Illinois is straightforward. After just a little data cleaning, we transformed it into date, time, and location columns of each fire starting from 2009 as shown in Figure A.2.

	C2	▾	f_x	1302 Hickory ST Champaign, IL	

	A	B	C
1	Alarm_Date	Alarm_Time	Address
2	1-Feb-09	14:29:03	1302 Hickory ST Champaign, IL
3	2-Feb-09	6:53:09	602 W Marketview DR Champaign, IL
4	15-Feb-09	20:13:33	1008 N Willis AVE Champaign, IL
5	17-Feb-09	21:48:00	902 E University AVE Champaign, IL
6	18-Feb-09	23:47:59	1703 W White ST Champaign, IL
7	28-Feb-09	18:42:31	409 Chalmers ST Champaign, IL
8	19-Mar-09	16:05:40	2003 W John ST Champaign, IL
9	24-Mar-09	20:26:16	401 E John ST Champaign, IL
10	5-Apr-09	11:35:52	621 Crescent DR Champaign, IL
11	6-Apr-09	15:27:52	1609 W Clark ST Champaign, IL
12	12-Apr-09	2:37:37	1203 S Fourth ST Champaign, IL
13	20-Apr-09	4:09:14	1519 Holly Hill DR Champaign, IL
14	7-May-09	15:00:26	308 S First ST Champaign, IL
15	9-May-09	14:30:40	2403 W Kirby AVE Champaign, IL
16	30-May-09	9:35:15	1401 N McKinley AVE Champaign, IL
17	1-Jun-09	14:51:20	304 E Hill ST Champaign, IL
18	15-Jun-09	11:43:35	53 E John ST Champaign, IL
19	30-Jun-09	5:55:52	1512 N Mattis AVE Champaign, IL
20	3-Jul-09	5:52:36	402 S Elm ST Champaign, IL
21	5-Jul-09	1:49:51	303 Holts DR Champaign, IL
22	6-Jul-09	11:26:41	1721 Henry ST Champaign, IL
23	11-Jul-09	2:15:52	57 E John ST Champaign, IL
24	23-Jul-09	3:37:46	2004 Sangamon DR Champaign, IL
25	24-Jul-09	10:37:58	505 E Armory AVE Champaign, IL
26	25-Jul-09	0:37:29	908 W Church ST Champaign, IL

Figure A.2

To upload the spreadsheet into Google Fusion Tables, we need to register a free Google Drive account to get file space online and Google Fusion. Once you have the Drive, all you have to do is click on it as shown in Figure A.3.

Figure A.3

When you have clicked on the drive, you will then click on "CREATE" and then choose Fusion Table in your options as in Figure A.4 (Sometimes you have to add Fusion Tables to your drive.)

Figure A.4

Once you have clicked on Fusion Table you will be taken to a screen that offers you the ability to connect to a file on your computer, on your Google Drive or from a website address or to create an empty table. In this case, we browsed our computer folders for the spreadsheet named ChampaignFiresReports. See Figure A.5.

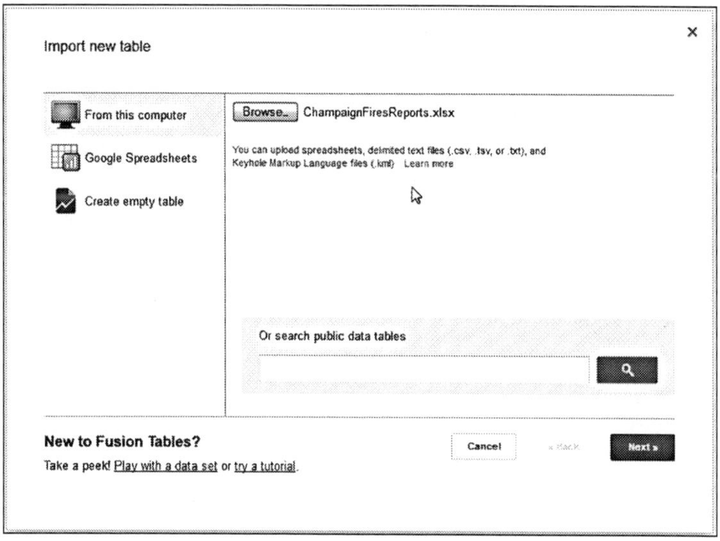

Figure A.5

We click on "Next" and it takes us a screen that shows the spreadsheet and we click on "Next" again as in Figure A.6.

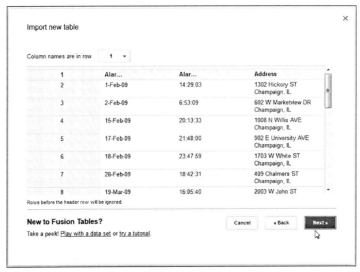

Figure A.6

The program then takes you to one last import screen shown in Figure A.7 where you can add notes about the file and then you hit "Finish."

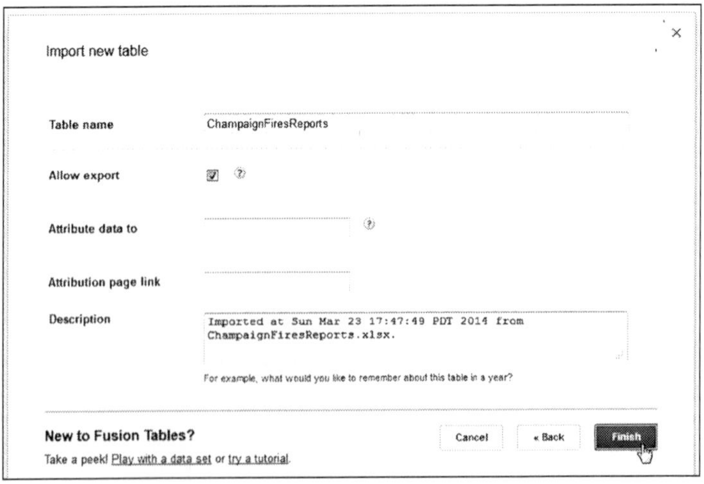

Figure A.7

When you click on "Finish" the file will import into Google Fusion Tables, initially showing up on the Rows tab that looks like the spreadsheet, but with the location automatically highlighted. (The program will always choose the likeliest column to be the location and sometimes you will have to choose a different column or rearrange your data.) See Figure A.8.

When you click on "Map of Address," the program will start "geocoding" the data, meaning

Figure A.8

it is matching the address with the template of geographical information—that is, with a map. This process happens in some form with every kind of mapping software. As you can see in Figure A.9, the program is also letting you know if any of the locations are ambiguous.

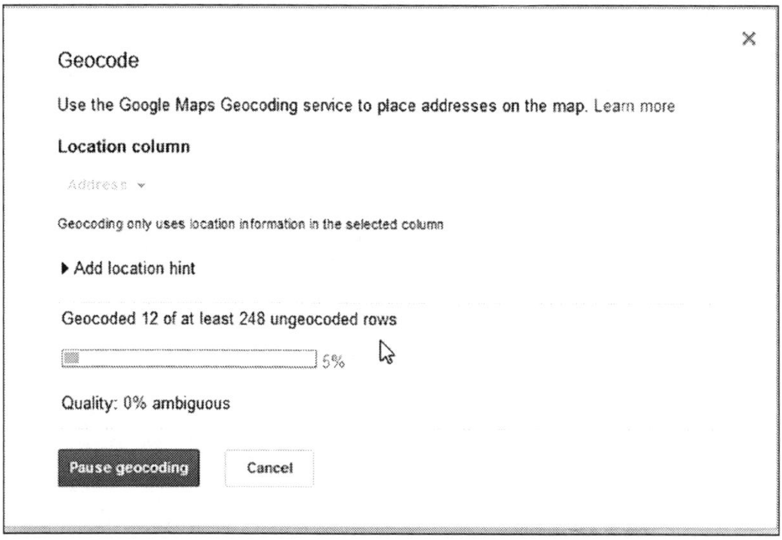

Figure A.9

When it is finished geocoding, it will show you a map that you may have to zoom in on, using the tool by the cursor. But now you have each fire in Champaign over the past 5 years visualized with a red dot on the map. This now allows you see patterns and if you want you can click on a dot to get the information about the fire as shown in Figure A.10.

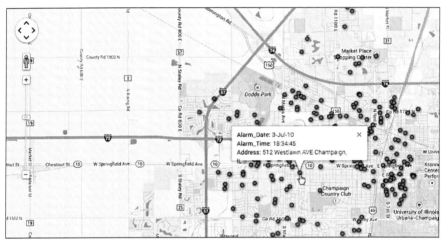

Figure A.10

If you want to see a more general pattern you can switch to "Heat Map," which does not represent the heat of the fire but represents clusters of fires through intensity of color. See Figure A.11.

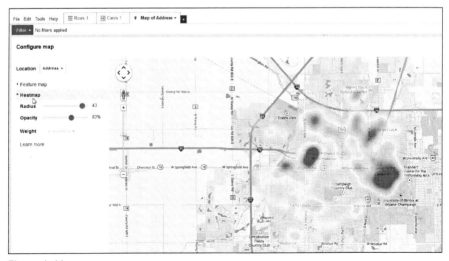

Figure A.11

Maps Using Different Location Data

Longitude and latitude data are often more reliable than street addresses. In this example, we will use ESRI Maps, which can be added to Microsoft Excel. The advantage of mapping with ESRI software is that it has been used by many governments and hundreds of thousands of people for years and there are many ready-made layers of maps for streets, rivers, terrain, and other geographical features.

In this case, we have data downloaded from the state of Illinois environmental website, which is about leaking underground storage tanks—usually old petroleum tanks—polluting the land water near them with gasoline or other products. The dataset is shown in Figure A.12.

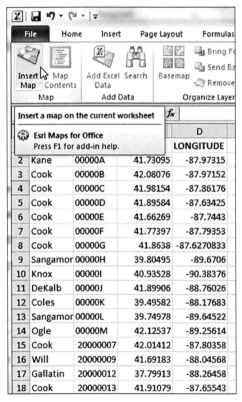

Figure A.12

So long as you are signed in with a user account, you can click on "Insert Map" and go to a screen where you can upload the data. You create a map by adding layers of maps from your files—in this case the leaking underground storage file in CSV format—or from existing basemaps as in Figure A.13.

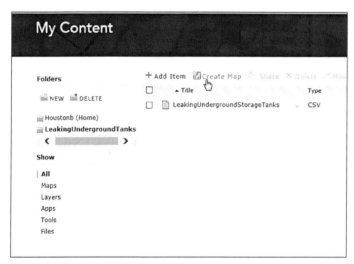

Figure A.13

After clicking on "Create a Map," you can upload your file by adding a layer and choosing the leaking tank data as in Figure A.14.

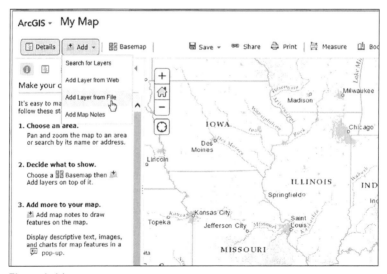

Figure A.14

When you add your file through the usual import procedure, you will get your dots identifying locations through longitude and latitude. You then can add a basemap of streets and highways as in Figure A.15.

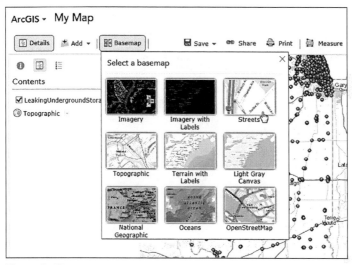

Figure A.15

When you click on the basemap of streets you will now see highways and zero streets and even streams in Figure A.16, which allows you to start reporting on clusters of leaking tanks and their proximity to water.

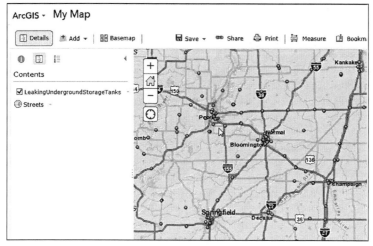

Figure A.16

Appendix B
A Short Introduction to Social Network Analysis

Throughout this book, we have looked at the most basic approaches to data analyses currently being used by journalists for producing stories. But there is an approach that journalists have begun to use more frequently from the social sciences: Social Network Analysis, a method for the analysis of social structure.

It is not surprising with the rise of social media, such as Facebook and Twitter, that this kind of analysis would gain new popularity and interest.

But one of the first uses of the technique was used in 1976 when journalists set out to investigate organized crime and public corruption in Phoenix, Arizona after a car bomb killed investigative reporter Don Bolles. During the investigation, known as the Arizona Project, journalists worked with a University of Arizona professor to illustrate the power of an informal group of politicians and businessmen, known as the Phoenix 40. The social network analysis provided the journalists with a social "road map" of the underpinnings of a corrupt system.

Social network analysis did not start becoming an integral part of CAR, however, until the early years of the 21st century. In one example, two University of Missouri graduate students, Jaimi Dowdell and Aaron Kessler, worked with *The Kansas City Star* in 2004 to show a network the U.S. government believed connected a relief agency, and alleged operative in Columbia, Missouri to terrorist Osama bin Laden.

In 2007 Ronald Campbell, then at *The Orange County Register*, used more than 10,000 pages of court records, financial reports, and other documents to show the network created by an imprisoned charity telemarketer to raise money for charities and "keep all but just 7 cents on the dollar for charity." He worked with a multimedia staff member, Geoffrey Anderson, to include an interactive social network analysis tool on the web, as shown in Figure B.1.

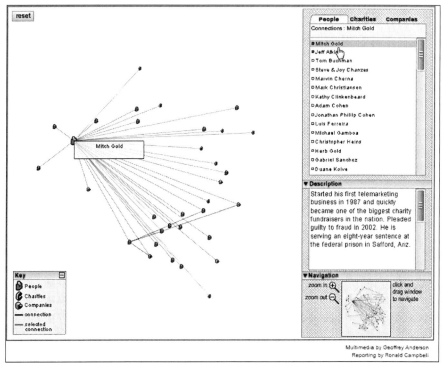

Figure B.1

"The Mitch Gold story was like a big ball of spaghetti: It involved dozens of characters, many companies and nonprofits (some of them legitimate, some of them fraudulent), several states," Campbell recalled.

"When I started, the only thing I knew was the person at the center: Mitch," Campbell said. "Social network analysis gave me a tool to link everything together and to understand which characters and companies were the most important and which ones were peripheral actors. That understanding in turn guided me when it came time to write the story."

The Organized Crime and Corruption Report, which uses network analysis routinely, has utilized it to follow international money laundering. As noted in Chapter 3, the Korean investigative journalism center used social network analysis to uncover Twitter accounts related to a government spy agency trying to influence elections.

In yet another example, *The Washington Post* used social network analysis in to report on a group of language schools in the Los Angeles area that appeared to be "visa mills" for foreign students. Using a database of a student visas, the newspaper showed that a total of 22 related language schools in the Los Angeles area had accounted for 33,000 visas issued, many good for up to 2 years.

Visualizing Relationships

Many other professions have been using social network analysis for some time. Among the users are business consultants, intelligence and law enforcement agencies, public health investigators, sociologists, and anthropologists.

Using free or inexpensive computer software such as NodeXL, Gephi, or Pajek, researchers look at social structures. The software and mathematical analysis basically allows the researcher to map relationships and the strength of those relationships and the placement of those relationships in the social structure being looked at.

As Ken Frank, who has taught the topic at Michigan State University, said, "Network analysis is based on the intuitive notion that these patterns are important features of the lives of the individuals who display them. Network analysts believe that how an individual lives depends in large part on how that individual is tied into the larger web of social connections."

The concepts of social network analysis began developing in the 1930s, but took a big leap ahead when computer graphics became available in the 1970s.

Quite often the data used for this approach is survey data. For example, public health researchers in Hartford, CT, tracked and mapped the relationships of who purchased heroin from whom and who injected it together and how race affected use. They gathered the data by surveying heroin users. The survey results were the dataset used in the network analysis.

Journalists and the public became more aware of this kind of analysis following the 2001 terrorist attacks against the World Trade Center. A practitioner of this method, business consultant Valdis E. Krebs, quickly outlined the possible relationships and organization of the 19 terrorists involved in the attack, using open sources—that is, information from newspapers—and was able to visually portray their contacts.

Krebs published an article, "Mapping Networks of Terrorist Cells," on his work with his own software computer-produced maps of relationships as shown in Figure B.2.

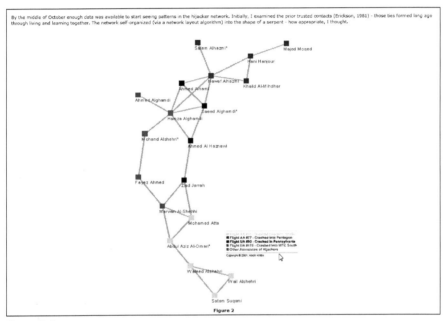

Figure B.2

Accompanying this diagram and others were color codes for each of the terrorists that noted which airline crash they were involved with. The diagrams showed which terrorist had met with which terrorist according to records in the public purview—newspaper clips and leaks from law enforcement. The diagram showed how infrequently contacts had been and who belonged to which terrorist cell. It also showed how isolated each cell could be to ensure secrecy.

This is a dramatic example of the use of social network analysis, but it shows the power to visualize relationships, especially in large data sets.

A Different Way to Look at Data

Like the other computer-assisted techniques you have learned, social network analysis has its own language and it can vary by software. Essentially, all software uses dots to represent persons or institutions and lines to represent the connections. In some software, these are called nodes and ties, or vertices and edges.

Social Network Analysis also looks at information differently than traditional columns and rows. In a regular worksheet, each column is a category of information and each row is a record. But in some social network software, a matrix is created in which every person and institution is listed in every row and every column, and when they are connected a cell is marked 1 and when not, it is marked 0.

But a version of social network analysis free software, NodeXL, is an add-on to Microsoft Excel and makes data entry a bit simpler.

After opening a NodeXL worksheet, we entered the fictional names of corporate executives who sit on various board of directors and the names of the companies on whose boards they sit. Their names are in Vertex 1 and the board they sit on is Vertex 2. Note the bottom of the screen, where it shows we are entering data in the Edges tab as shown in Figure B.3.

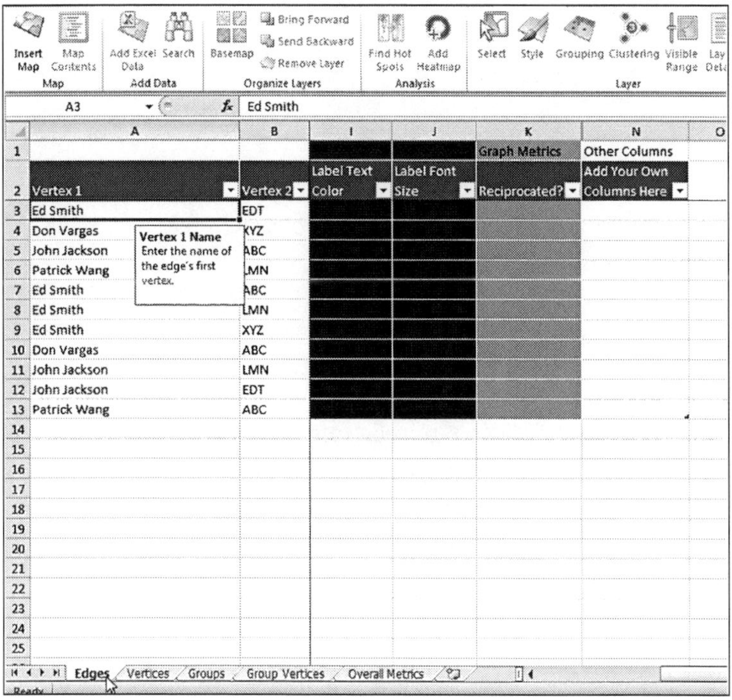

Figure B.3

If we move to the Vertices tab at the bottom of the screen, we see the program allows us to label the Vertices with names as shown in Figure B.4 so they will show up on our eventual diagram.

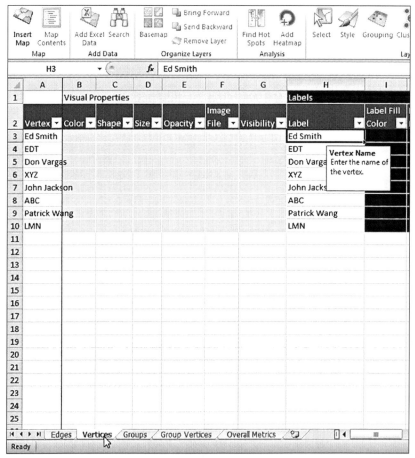

Figure B.4

Once we have all our names entered we put them into a graph or diagram. There are several steps involved, but you can see the rudimentary diagram we can produce without too much work as shown in Figure B.5.

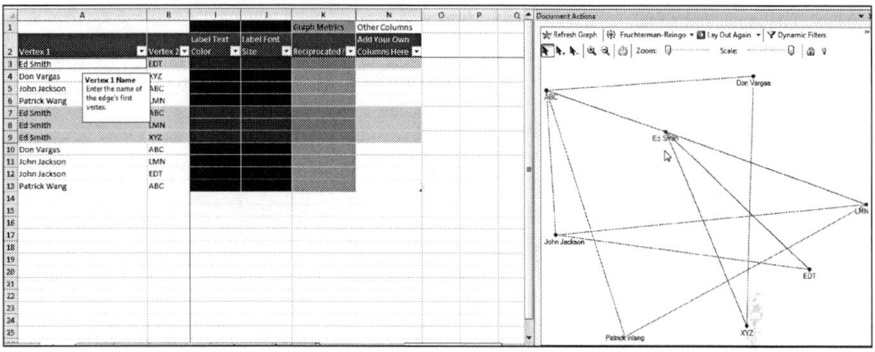

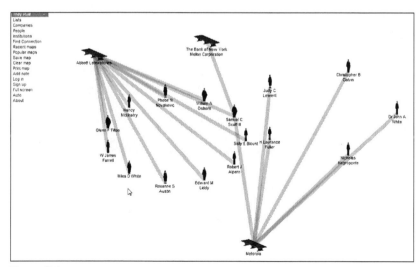

Figure B.5

As you can easily see in this small dataset, some of these executives sit on the board of each other's companies with Ed Smith sitting on the most boards.

In recent years, business reporters have delved into questions raised by interlocking directorships on boards and potential conflict of interests. One famous project was "TheyRule," which looked at 100 corporate boards with a very easy to use interactive tool as shown in Figure B.6.

Figure B.6

Another website, Muckety.com, was created by journalists and technologists to do social network analysis. It has since gone out of business, but the About page gave a good overview of what they did, as in Figure B.7.

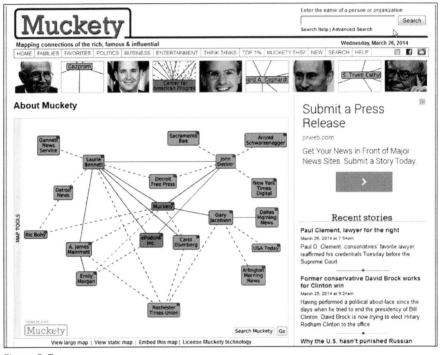

Figure B.7

Depending on the dataset and the analysis, social network analysis maps can go far beyond the diagrams shown so far. Experts use mathematical techniques to determine the importance of a person or entity in a network and to measure the distance and closeness of relationships. You could see how many degrees of separation there are.

Even basic use of this analysis can be helpful in understanding how decisions and policies are made. It shows how people interact and what patterns evolve through these interactions, which is what journalists observe and write about every day. Again, it requires more than seeing connections. It involves interviews and understanding the strength of a connection and its real influence.

But applying these techniques to your community, you could start to more closely track who knows whom, who is isolated from the powerful and disenfranchised, and who is related to whom. With a better understanding of the relationships, you could ask more probing questions or even prepare better for a routine interview.

Selected Bibliography

Berret, Charles, and Cheryl Phillips, *Teaching Data and Computational Journalism*. New York, NY: Columbia University, 2016.

Cairo, Albert. *The Functional Art: An Introduction to Information Graphics and Visualization*. Berkeley, CA: New Riders, 2013.

Cohen, Sarah. *Numbers in the Newsroom: Using Math and Statistics in News*. Columbia, MO: Investigative Reporters and Editors, 2014.

Cuillier, David, and Charles N. Davis. *The Art of Access: Strategies for Acquiring Public Records*. Washington, DC: CQ, 2011.

Egawhary, Elena, and Cynthia O'Murchu. *Data Journalism* (handbook). The Centre for Investigative Journalism. http://tcij.org/resources/handbooks/data-journalism.

Gray, Jonathan, Liliana Bounegru, and Lucy Chamber, eds. *The Data Journalism Handbook: How Journalists Can Use Data to Improve the News*. Sebastopol, CA: O'Reilly Media, 2012. http://datajournalismhandbook.org/1.0/en/.

Houston, Brant, and Investigative Reporters and Editors, eds. *The Investigative Reporter's Handbook: A Guide to Documents, Databases, and Techniques*. 5th ed. Boston, MA: Bedford/St. Martin's, 2009.

Huff, Darrell. *How to Lie with Statistics*. New York, NY: W.W. Norton, 1993.

Ingram, Matthew. "The Golden Age of Computer-Assisted Reporting Is At Hand," *Nieman Journalism Lab*, May 20, 2009. www.niemanlab.org/2009/05/the-golden-age-of-computer-assisted-reporting-is-at-hand/.

Jones, Gerald Everett. *How to Lie with Charts*. 2nd ed. Santa Monica, CA: LaPuerta, 2007.

Method, Jason. "The Benefits of Computer-Assisted Reporting," *Nieman Reports*, Fall 2008. http://nieman.harvard.edu/reports/article/100454/The-Benefits-of-Computer-Assisted-Reporting.aspx.

Meyer, Philip. *Precision Journalism: A Reporter's Introduction to Social Science Methods*. 4th ed. Lanham, MD: Rowman & Littlefield, 2002.

Monmonier, Mark. *How to Lie with Maps*. 2nd ed. Chicago, IL: University of Chicago Press, 1996.

Paulos, John Allen. *Beyond Numeracy: Ruminations of a Numbers Man*. New York, NY: Vintage, 1992.

Tufte, Edward R. *Envisioning Information*. Cheshire, CT: Graphics, 1990.

Vallance-Jones, Fred, and David McKie; with Aron Pilhofer and Jaimi Dowdell. *Computer-Assisted Reporting: A Comprehensive Primer*. Don Mills, ON; New York, NY: Oxford University Press, 2009.

Winkleman, Simon, ed. *Data Journalism in Asia: A Collection of Articles From Members of the Society of Asian Journalists (AJ)*. Singapore: Konrad-Adenauer-Stiftung, 2013. www.kas.de/wf/doc/kas_35547–1522-2-30.pdf?130930105417.

Websites

African News Innovation Challenge. http://africannewschallenge.org
Association of Public Data Users. http://apdu.org
Center for Investigative Reporting. www.revealnews.org/
Center for Responsive Politics. www.opensecrets.org
Centre for Investigative Journalism. http://tcij.org
Columbia Journalism Review, Data Points, Exploring Data Journalism. www.cjr.org/data_points/
Data Driven Journalism, Where Journalism Meets Data. http://datadrivenjournalism.net
Data Journalism Blog. www.datajournalismblog.com
Data Journalism Blog, Paul Bradshaw's blog. www.datajournalismblog.com/tag/paul-bradshaw/
Data.gov. www.data.gov
Global Investigative Journalism Network, Data Journalism. http://gijn.org/resources/data-journalism/
The Google News Initiative. https://newsinitiative.withgoogle.com/
The Guardian, Data Journalism. www.theguardian.com/media/data-journalism
Guidestar. www.guidestar.org
International Consortium of Investigative Journalists, Computer-Assisted Reporting. www.icij.org/tags/computer-assisted-reporting
Investigative Reporters and Editors, Resource Center. www.ire.org/resource-center/
LexisNexis. www.lexisnexis.com
National Institute for Computer-Assisted Reporting. www.ire.org/nicar/
National Institute on Money in State Politics. www.followthemoney.org
NewsBank. www.newsbank.com
ProPublica, Journalism in the Public Interest. www.ProPublica.org

Pulitzer Prizes. www.pulitzer.org

R, The R Project for Statistical Computing. www.r-project.org

Reporters Committee for Freedom of the Press. www.rcfp.org

Research Clinic, Investigative Research Links and Articles by Paul Myers. http://researchclinic.net

SearchSystems.net, Free Public Records. www.searchsystems.net

UNdata. http://data.un.org

United Network for Organ Sharing. www.unos.org

U.S. Bureau of Alcohol, Tobacco, Firearms and Explosives. www.atf.gov

U.S. Census Bureau. www.census.gov

U.S. Government Accountability Office. www.gao.gov

The World Health Organization. http://www.who.int/gho/database/en/

Sources for Key Examples

The examples at the beginning of the chapters and in the "Applying CAR" sections were selected from *Uplink*, the newsletter and blog on computer-assisted reporting created and maintained by Investigative Reporters and Editors and the National Institute for Computer-Assisted Reporting at www.ire.org/blog/uplink/ and from presentations at conferences.

Glossary

Address—In a spreadsheet, the location (cell) on a worksheet identified by a letter and number.

Algorithm—A computer code that is a process or a set of rules to solve a problem or carry out a task such as social media sites' algorithms that ranks a users' interest in a various posts.

Ascending—Sorting low to high.

ASCII—American Standard Code for Information Interchange. Pronounced ASK-KEY. A file that looks like a text file and can be read by almost any software program.

Average—Usually means the total amount divided by the number of items making up the amount, but in math can refer to mean, median, and mode.

Boolean Logic—A way of searching online and in database managers that used the words *and, or,* and *not* to filter information.

Bot—A software application that runs automated tasks over the internet such as an application imitating a human being conversing.

Browser—Software that allows you to see and read web pages.

Byte—A measure of amount of space on store that is composed of eight bits.

Cell—In a spreadsheet, a box containing information.

Codebook—A document translating codes in a database.

Columns—Categories of information in a worksheet.

Comma-Separated Values—Known as CSV, this data format separates columns by commas or other punctuation. This commonly used format compacts a dataset, but is easily opened by spreadsheets and other software.

Computational Journalism—A kind of data journalism focused on the use of algorithms in reporting.

Computer-Assisted reporting—Finding and analyzing databases as a part of part of the reporting process.

Data Journalism—Frequently a catch-all phrase for data analysis and visual presentations.

Database—A file or collection of related files, sometimes known as tables.

Database Manager—A software program that organizes information in a database.

Descending—Sorting high to low.

Dirty Data—Data that has been incorrectly entered into a dataset through typos or miscoding.

Downloading—To transfer files to your own computer from a computer you have contacted online.

Enterprise Matchmaking—Joining databases that have not been set up to be joined.

Field—A category of information like a column in a spreadsheet.

Filter—To select a subset of numbers from a larger set.

From Statement—An SQL statement that chooses which database or table to look at.

Google Groups—A group of people interested in the same topic who receive and send email to those in the group.

Group by Statement—An SQL statement that divides records into groups based on identical fields.

Grouping—Dividing similar data into groups.

Having Statement—A statement that selects records by a criteria after they have been grouped. Acts like "where" does on individual records in SQL.

LexisNexis—A large commercial database of newspaper clippings and court cases.

Listserv—A discussion group on the internet on a particular topic. All messages sent to the listserv go to all those who have joined.

Mapping Software—Software, known as Geographical Information Systems, that produces maps by matching templates such as street addresses to data filed imported into the software.

Matches/Hits—Finding identical information in the key fields of two or more files, or tables, in a relational database.

Mean—The same as average.

Median—An average that is the middle value in a series of numbers. Half of the numbers are higher and half are lower than the median.

Mode—An average that is the number most often occurring in a series of numbers. For example, the most frequent (not majority) salary in a group of people would be the mode.

Observation—A record in statistical software.

Order by Statement—A SQL statement that sorts the records based on one or more fields.

Outliers—Numbers at the extreme of a series of numbers.

Parsing—Dividing a column into one or more columns or information in the columns.

Percentage—The proportion of one number to another.

Percentage Difference—A proportion of change between two columns of numbers.

Pivot Table—A table of information that allows you to both total numbers in different groups and calculate the percentage of the total those numbers make up. Similar to "group by" in database managers.

Portable Document Format—Known as PDF, it formats files and data in a rigid way that must be converted to a spreadsheet or other formats so that data in it can be analyzed.

Query—A way in a database manager to select, filter, group, and sort information in a database.

Rates—The number of occurrences divided by the population in which the occurrences happen, such as 12 murders per 100,000 persons.

Ratio—One number divided by another to give a sense of proportion, such as 3 to 1.

Record—A row of information in a database manager.

Record Layout—Information about the names and size of fields in a database.

Relational Databases—Databases composed of tables that can be joined through "key fields."

Rows—Individual records in a worksheet.

Scraping—Using software to download data and information and importing into a database.

Search Tool—A program that allows you to search for information on the internet.

Searchers—Experts who know how to find information on the internet.

Select Statement—A statement in SQL that selects the fields (or columns) to look at.

Sort—Organizing data from high to low based information in a column.

Spreadsheet—Software program often used for calculations, budgets, and other number-related tasks or to filter or organize datasets.

SQL—Structured Query Language. A language used for doing queries in a database and reorganizing and recoding data.

Summary Data—Data that has been divided into groups and totaled.

Tables—Files used by database managers.

Tabular—Information in a table of columns and rows.

URL—Uniform Resource Locator. The address of a website.

Variable—A category of information in statistical software.

Where Statement—A statement in SQL that selects by a criteria the records to look at within a database.

Zip—To compress a file so that information can be stored and transferred more efficiently.

Index

accuracy: cleaning dirty data 14, 1
75–178; dirty data 12, 14, 165–176;
importance of xiv, 2, 12, 57, 74, 132,
154, 163; mean, median, and mode
74
Adopt-A-Highway database 142
The Akron Beacon-Journal (Ohio) 179
American Banker 23
analysis software, evolution of, 9
anchoring cells, in spreadsheets
69–71
"and", in Boolean logic 26, 116
APDU (Association for Public Data
Users) 138–139
Arc Online 10, 193
The Arkansas Democrat-Gazette 40
Asbury Park Press (New Jersey) 135
ascending sort, in spreadsheets 72
The Atlanta Journal-Constitution
(Georgia) 8, 121, 132
auditors' reports, finding data in
138
average, mean in spreadsheets 74

bail data, analysis of 77, 92
Barlett, Donald 8
Bengtsson, Helena 149
Berens, Mike 23–24, 152
Berners-Lee, Tim 1
Bolles, Don 205

Boolean logic: internet searches and 26;
use in database managers for criteria
110, 116–117; use in spreadsheets for
filtering 86–88
Borowski, Neill 74
Bristol Herald Courier (Virginia) 4
Brown, James 8

Callicoat, Jason 181
Campbell, Ronald 205–206
CAR *see* computer-assisted reporting
Carter, Edward 15–16, 182
CBS, computer-based electoral
predictions by 7
Census Bureau *see* U.S. Census
Bureau
central number, use in writing story
187
The Charleston Gazette (West Virginia)
100–101
The Charlotte Observer (North Carolina)
130
charts, spreadsheet tools for 97–99
code sheet 15, 140–142, 144, 165–166,
168–170
Cohen, Sarah 80, 187
The Columbus Dispatch (Ohio) 23–24,
103, 152
commands, in Structured Query
Language (SQL) 110

comma separated value (CSV) files 21, 28–29, 33–35, 37–38,145, 182, 202; importing data using 144–146
commercial records 6, 136
computer-assisted reporting (CAR): basic tools 9–10; defined 4; history of 7–9; learning guidelines for 11; summary of steps in 189–190; writing guidelines 187–188; see also specific tools for CAR
cost, issues for database access 143–144
The Courant see The Hartford Courant
The Courier-Post (New Jersey) 79
crime statistics 152; construction of database on 151; FBI data 80, 156, 166, 177; rates in 80–84
criteria: in database management 113–114; in spreadsheets 88–89
cryptic codes, in databases 168–170
CSV file see comma-separated value (CSV) files
curiosity, reporting based on 188
Curtis, Hanque 161

Dalton, Richard J. 19
Daniels, Frank III 6
data analysis, basic principles of xiv
database managers 10; Boolean logic in 116–117; concept of 19; database construction using 154–158; DB Browser SQLite 10, 18, 103; "group by" 110, 118–120; matchmaking ("join" statements) 123–130; Microsoft Access 10, 13, 103; "order by" 110, 114–118; queries 109, 120; Query by Example 13, 105, 125; "select" 110, 112–115; Table Design 154–158; "where" (criteria) 110, 114–116; see also relational databases
data dictionary see code sheet
data entry clerks, engaging with 138
Data.gov 27, 181

data journalism: basic techniques 9–10; history of 7–10
The Dayton Daily News (Ohio) 132
DB Browser, SQLite: campaign contributions analysis using 107–121; linked table creation 129–133; wildcards 117–118
"Deadly Force" (Washington Post series) 177
DeBarros, Anthony 152
delimited files 28
descending sort, in spreadsheets 72
Deseret News (Utah) 16, 182
The Detroit Free Press 8
digital information sources 23–26
digital library researchers 25
dirty data 14, 161–176; kinds of pitfalls 165
discussion groups 9, 21, 25–26
DocumentCloud 43, 46–49
Doig, Steve 10, 130, 194
Dowdell, Jaimi 205
downloading and opening guidelines 29–36

The Eagle-Tribune (Massachusetts) 130
edges, in social network analysis 209
Ellis, Joe 190–191
enterprise matchmaking, relational databases 127–129
Erickson, John 132
ESRI software (mapping) 10, 139, 193, 201–203
ethics, reporting with data 188
EveryBlock organization (dirty data) 163
Ewing, Jack 77, 188
Excel files see spreadsheets
Eyre, Eric 100–101

Facebook 25, 50–56, 205
fact-checking 24–27

Federal Election Commission (FEC) 104, 108, 126, 171
fieldwork, importance of 188
file types 28
filtering: database management 113–115; spreadsheet applications for 86–89
Fine, Scott 100–101
"first ventures" stories 181–182
Fish, Mike 121
fixed format files 28; downloading guidelines 29–33; importing data using 144–146
flat file, relational database construction and 156
Foundation Center (New York) 40
Frank, Ken 207
"from" command (SQL) 110

GAO (Government Accountability Office) 138
geocoding 200
geographical information systems (GIS) 9–10, 138, 193
Gephi software 10, 207
Gilbert, Daniel 4
GIS see geographical information systems (GIS)
Global Investigative Journalism Network 8, 139, 180, 185
Gold, Mitch 206
Goldstein, Brad 130
Google Drive 196–197
Google Fusion Tables 10, 193, 195–199
Google Groups 25
Google search: advanced search for databases 19–20; Boolean logic and 26–27
Government Accountability Office (GAO) 138
government databases 24; access to 136–139; costs of 143; downloading from 27; linked tables in 13, 123;

obtaining 139–141; privacy and security issues and 146, 147; see also specific organizations and databases
graphs, spreadsheet tools for 97–100
Greenblatt, Mark 182
Greene, Robert W. 184
grid see spreadsheets
"group by" command (SQL) 110
grouping, in database managers 118–119
The Guardian 9, 10, 185, 194–195
Guidestar organization 40

Hacks/Hackers group 186
Haddix, Doug 52
hardcopy reports 170
hardware 137, 139, 186
The Hartford Courant (Connecticut) 60, 77, 143, 150, 183
"having" command (SQL) 110
hazardous materials transportation database 126
headers, in databases 39, 72, 154, 165, 173–174
heat map 200
Helms, Jesse 6
hits, in enterprise matching 130
Holovaty, Adrian 163
horizontal rows, in spreadsheets 22, 67
Houser, Mark 182
Howard, Alexander Benjamin 1
HTML files 28
HyperText Markup Language (HTML) see HTML files

Idsvoog, Karl 183
importing data, guidelines for 31–36, 144–146
Internal Revenue Service (IRS) 40–41
International Consortium of Investigative Journalists 4

international journalists, computer-assisted reporting by 180–181

Investigative Reporters and Editors (IRE) i, 8, 180–181, 185

Investigative Reporter's Handbook (Houston) 24

IRE *see* Investigative Reporters and Editors (IRE)

The IRE Journal 185

IRS database 40–41

Jaspin, Elliot 5, 8, 170

Johnson, Corky 183

Jones, Daniel 183

journalist-programmers, history of 9, 186

Justice Department *see* U.S. Justice Department

The Kansas City Star (Missouri) 23, 205

Kessler, Aaron 205

key fields: database construction and 158; in databases 125–128

Knox, David 179

Krebs, Valdis E. 208

LaFleur, Jennifer 142

Landau, George 163

latitudinal data, mapping with 194, 201–203,

LexisNexis database 23, 25, 180

"like" function, database management 115–116

LinkedIn 25, 50, 52

linked tables 13, 123

Linsk, Rick 146–147

Lipton, Eric 43, 46, 60–62

listservs 25–26, 39

local police databases 3, 150–151, 177

longitudinal data, mapping with 201–203

Los Angeles Times 163

"lurking variables" in stories 188

Maier, Thomas 19

mainframe systems, computer-assisted reporting and 7–9

mainstream journalism, computer-assisted reporting and 5

mapping software 9–11, 193, 195, 199

McGinty, Jo Craven 150, 177

McGinty, Tom 27

mean, in spreadsheets 74–76

median, in spreadsheets 74–76

Meitrodt, Jeffrey 158–159

Method, Jason 135

Meyer, Philip 5, 8, 79

Miami Herald (Florida) 8, 10, 130, 194

Microsoft Access 10, 13, 21, 103, 105, 121, 125, 145, 195; building a database in 154–157; *see also* databases; specific commands

Microsoft ESRI Maps *see* ESRI software (mapping)

Microsoft Excel *see* spreadsheets

minimum story strategy 15, 153, 184–185, 187

Missouri School of Journalism 8, 9, 182

mode, in spreadsheets 74

Morin, Rich 8

Mullins, Richard 21–22

Myers, Paul 25, 52

National Institute for Computer-Assisted Reporting (NICAR) 8, 15, 26, 142–143, 176, 181, 185, 186, 190; listserv 26, 185

National Public Radio (NPR) 25

NewsBank 25

news-clipping library, online sources 23–24

Newsday 19

newsroom databases 25

The New York Times 25, 43, 60, 123, 177, 187

NICAR *see* National Institute for Computer-Assisted Reporting (NICAR)
Nine Track Express program 8
nodes, in social network analysis 209
NodeXL 10, 207, 209
Nordberg, Jenny 149
"not", in Boolean logic 26

offensive characters, in databases 175
online resources 9–11; guidelines for using 23–25; kinds 9; purposes 21; reliability of 24
Open Calais 11, 47, 49
The Orange County Register 205–206
"or", in Boolean logic 26
"order by" command (SQL) 110
Organized Crime and Corruption Report 207
The Orlando Sentinel 161
outer integrity checks 164, 170
outliers, interpretation of 76; *see also* "group by" command (SQL)

Pajek software 207
parity in journalism, computer–assisted reporting and 5
parsing, in databases 176, 184
parts to the sum comparisons 69–71
pattern recognition 5, 11, 24, 43–44, 59, 77–78, 119, 120, 152, 154–155, 166, 187, 188, 194, 197, 199, 200, 207; *see also* relationships, social network analysis of
patterns in spreadsheets *see* spreadsheets
PDF *see* portable document format (PDF)
percentage calculations, in spreadsheets 64–6
personal computers, computer-assisted reporting and 8

The Philadelphia Inquirer 8, 74
Phoenix (Arizona Project) 205
The Pittsburgh Tribune-Review (Pennsylvania) 79, 182
pivot tables, spreadsheet applications for 90–97
political contributors, database construction for 154–158
portable document format (PDF) 22, 28
Porter, Jeff 40–41
Precision Journalism (Meyer) 5, 8, 79
primary resources, online sources for 24
privacy issues, database access and 142–143; *see also* security issues
programming 9, 176, 186
The Providence Journal-Bulletin (Rhode Island) 8, 170
public information, electronic access to 135–136
Pulitzer Prizes 8, 60, 80, 150, 177, 194
Python software 9, 176

queries 109; building 109–115; by example 105, 125; *see also* Structured Query Language (SQL)

R (software) 79, 138
racial disparities: analysis of 10, 77–78
The Raleigh News & Observer 6, 186
ranking, spreadsheet tools for 84–86
rates, in spreadsheets 80–84
ratios, in spreadsheets 89–90
record layout 140–142
relational databases 104, 125–132; creating 156–158; SQL 10, 13, 110, 126, 172; SQLite 10, 103, 105, 145, 155
relationships, social network analysis of 207–213
research, online resources for 8, 20
Research Clinic 52
researchers, journalists as 25

salary comparisons, spreadsheet tools for 62–76

SAS software 10, 79, 138

search and replace instructions 175

search engines: Boolean logic and 26–27; *see also* specific search engines

searching strategies 26

The Seattle Times (Washington) 152

secondary resources, online sources for 24

security issues 142–143, 150

"select" command (SQL) 110

September 11, 2001, terrorist attacks 3; database on victims of 152; social network analysis following 208

shifting information, record layout miscues and 167–168

social media: kinds 50; research using 25–26; search tools 52

social network analysis 9, 55–57; nodes in 209; use for stories 205–213

Social Security number, relational databases and use of 125

sorting techniques: in database managers 114; in spreadsheets 71–73, 95

South, Jeff 59

The South Bend Tribune (Indiana) 181

sports salaries, spreadsheet analysis of 74–76

spreadsheets 9, 12–13; addresses on 62–64; average and median for accuracy on 74–76; charts and graphs 97–100; database construction with 158; data searches for 20; filtering functions 86–89; guidelines for using 59–60; horizontal and vertical rows on 67–69; math skills for using 60; mean in 74–76; median in 74–76; mode in 74; outlier interpretation 76–77; parts to sum comparisons on 69–71; percentage calculations 64–66; pivot tables 90–97; ranking

applications using 84–86; rates in 80–84; ratios in 89–90; sorting results on 71–73; VLookup 172–173; *see also* specific types of spreadsheets

SPSS software 10, 79, 138

SQL *see* Structured Query Language (SQL)

standards, lack of in databases 165, 171–174

The Star-Ledger (Newark, New Jersey) 123

statistical software 9–10, 79

Steele, James 8

Stith, Pat 185

storage space, growth of 2

The St. Paul Pioneer Press 146–147

string functions 176

structured data 19

Structured Query Language (SQL) 105: commands 110; data cleaning using 175–176; linked table creation 125–131; *see also* specific commands

sum function: in database manager grouping 68–69; parts to the sum comparisons 69–71; in pivot tables 90–97

Supplementary Homicide Report 177

survey data, social network analysis and 207

Tableau 9, 10, 16, 180, 193

text: in databases 154; files 28, 31–36, 176; unstructured data 19, 44

"TheyRule" project 211

ties (social network analysis) in data 209

The Times Picayune (New Orleans, Louisiana) 60, 158–159

Transportation Security Administration database 3

trend recognition 52, 60

Tumblr 50

Twitter 50: searching 50–52; trend searching 52
two-dimensional world, in data searching 22

United Nations 28, 181
United Network for Organ Sharing 37
unstructured data 4, 11, 12, 19; using DocumentCloud 47–49; visualizing 44–46
"update" command (SQL), data cleaning using 172–173
Uplink 181
USA Today 60, 152
U.S. Census Bureau 28, 191
U.S. Justice Department 143

validation rules 157, 162
vertices, in social network analysis 209–210
visualization 12, 14; database manager, joining 125; spreadsheet tools for 97–99; unstructured data 44–46
VLOOKUP formula 172–173
voter registration data, record layout miscues in 168

Walton Family Foundation 40–41
The Washington Post (Washington, D.C.) 4, 25, 150, 177, 207
The Waterbury Republican American (Connecticut) 81
web scraping 9, 37–40
"where" command (SQL) 110; filtering 113–114; linked table creation 125–127
wildcards: using 114–116, 174; in database management 114–115; data cleaning and 174
Williams, Margot 25
wizard screens, downloading and opening guidelines 28–32
Wolf, Barnet D. 103
Woods, Daniel 8
Word Clouds 44–46
World Bank data 181
World Health Organization data 29, 181
writing guidelines, for computer-assisted reporting 187–188

ZIP codes, format in databases 154, 175

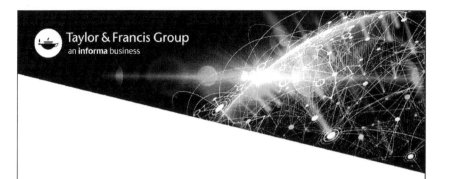